How We See Us

Work and Learning Series

Series edited by Robert B. Schwartz and Nancy Hoffman

OTHER BOOKS IN THIS SERIES
Schooling in the Workplace
Nancy Hoffman

Youth, Education, and the Role of Society
Robert Halpern

Learning for Careers
Nancy Hoffman and Robert B. Schwartz

Vocational Education and Training for a Global Economy
Edited by Marc S. Tucker

Career Pathways in Action
Edited by Robert B. Schwartz and Amy Loyd

Career Pathways for All Youth
Stephen F. Hamilton

Teaching Students About the World of Work
Edited by Nancy Hoffman and Michael Lawrence Collins

America's Hidden Economic Engines
Edited by Robert B. Schwartz and Rachel Lipson

Who Needs College Anymore?
Kathleen deLaski

How We See Us

Young People Imagining a Path to Their Futures

MICHAELA M. LESLIE-RULE

HARVARD EDUCATION PRESS
CAMBRIDGE, MASSACHUSETTS

Copyright © 2025 by the President and Fellows of Harvard College

All rights reserved. No part of this publication may be reproduced or transmitted in any form or by any means, electronic or mechanical, including photocopy, recording, or any information storage and retrieval systems, without permission in writing from the publisher.

Paperback ISBN 978-1-68253-979-8

Library of Congress Cataloging-in-Publication Data
Names: Leslie-Rule, Michaela Maria, author.
Title: How we see us : young people imagining a path to their futures / Michaela M. Leslie-Rule.
Other titles: Work and learning series.
Description: Cambridge, Massachusetts : Harvard Education Press, [2025] | Series: Work and
    learning series | Includes bibliographical references and index.
Identifiers: LCCN 2024047626 | ISBN 9781682539798 (paperback)
Subjects: LCSH: Youth—United States—Attitudes. | Youth—United States—Psychology. |
    African American youth—Attitudes. | African American youth—Psychology. | Hispanic American
    youth—Attitudes. | Hispanic American youth—Psychology. | Poor youth—United States—
    Attitudes. | Poor youth—United States—Psychology. | Youth development—United States. |
    Youth—Employment—United States. | Education—United States.
Classification: LCC HQ796 .L3844 2025 | DDC 305.2350973—dc23/eng/20241125
LC record available at https://lccn.loc.gov/2024047626

Published by Harvard Education Press,
an imprint of the Harvard Education Publishing Group

Harvard Education Press
8 Story Street
Cambridge, MA 02138

Cover by Dave Kessler Design

The typefaces in this book are Adobe Garamond Pro and Myriad Pro.

For Desta Oliver and Cramon Oliver,
and the ninety years between them.

Contents

	Series Editor Foreword	ix
	Nancy Hoffman	
	Work and Learning Series Editor	
	Preface	xiii
INTRODUCTION	The "Why" and the "What" of This Book	1
CHAPTER 1	Vignettes: Young People, Uninterrupted	13
CHAPTER 2	Listening to One Group in New York	39
CHAPTER 3	What It Looks Like to Build Your Own Pathway	51
CHAPTER 4	Conversation as Intervention	77
CHAPTER 5	Guidance, Frameworks, and Parting Thoughts	91
	Acknowledgments	111
	Appendix A: Methodology	113
	Appendix B: Worksheet: Mapping Life and Career Pathways with Young People	125
	Notes	131
	About the Author	137
	Index	139

Series Editor Foreword

NANCY HOFFMAN

WORK AND LEARNING SERIES EDITOR

How We See Us makes three challenging pleas, each of which Michaela Leslie-Rule owns for herself as well as addresses to her caring readers. First, she asks that we not buy into the crisis and trauma narrative that declares Black and Hispanic young people and young people from lower-income households in trouble; second, that we not lose sight of individuals when aggregating data into categories and frameworks; and third, and perhaps most important, that we treat these three groups of young people as we would our own children. The young people the author listened to in myriad focus groups, and whose life maps she analyzed for the underlying research project, are unequivocal: Black and Hispanic young people want freedom to explore the adult world of work as they develop their occupational identities. We should not push them to find a career path prematurely and follow it purely because we fear they will be treated unfairly by our education, workforce, and social systems based on their race or because they come from families experiencing poverty.

But Leslie-Rule is also a pragmatist. A particularly compelling aspect of this book is the courage and honesty the author displays in recognizing the conundrum of categorization when centering individual youth voices. She may, as she notes, caution against aggregating data into frameworks and categories, but she also knows that these can be helpful. And she wants this book to impact practice. For example, she and her research partner *did* construct what I find an exceedingly helpful framework. Leslie-Rule introduces this framework (No. 1, chapter 5) thus: "I've shared how most of the young people with whom we spoke were optimistic about their future lives. Most young people we talked to believed they would thrive in the future. Where we saw differences among young people was in how well-equipped they felt to set goals for themselves, and how confident they were that they either possessed or could locate the information, resources, and people they thought they might need to achieve their goals."

Accordingly, the *Five Occupational Pathways* (pages 53 and 98) moves within a continuum that characterizes young people in relation to their occupational identity development. The Pathways vividly illustrate and suggest categories to understand how young people see themselves developing their career and work identities and how confident or aware they are of not only what they want to do but of the steps they can take and explore to get there. I have found these pathway categories helpful in my own work, but I do keep Leslie-Rule's caution in mind. She addresses her readers in the second person on page 99: "It can be tempting to use the occupational pathways exercise prescriptively—a classification system for students. Don't do this . . . Think of it more as something you have in your back pocket."

Finally, and in keeping with the author's honesty, only after the research is over and Leslie-Rule is listening again to the transcripts of young voices, does she validate a positive unintended and surprising consequence of the focus groups: the young people in the focus groups listened intently to each other, jumped in to provide peers, unknown an hour earlier, with advice, encouragement, and ideas. These young people unhesitatingly "lifted each other up," sometimes exchanging contact information and offering to help one another to be accountable to their goals. At the close of one group's meeting in New York, Ali says what many appeared to be thinking: "More of us should be talking to more people. Because, like,. . . . I grew from this conversation alone" (page 82).

I hope that in these few paragraphs, you've gotten the flavor of this important book. As the cocurator of the Work and Learning Series and the author of several books in the series myself, I am so pleased that this book will see the light of day at a moment when the country should be hungry for a hopeful look at what seem intractable problems of poverty, inequality, and outright racism. *How We See Us* has a special place in the series.

While these themes permeate the other eight books in the series, including most recently, *Teaching Students about the World of Work* (2019) and *America's Hidden Economic Engines* (2023), *How We See Us* is one of only two books in which young people's experience is the heart of the matter.[1]

Interestingly, the two books directly foregrounding the experience of older adolescents and young adults bookend a decade of work to provide better options and more equitable outcomes for young people. The vehicles are primarily effective and appealing career pathways education for all. Other books, however, address our readers with analyses and case studies focused on improving institutions that serve learners experiencing poverty or showcasing successful systemic interventions in career education to increase their economic mobility in the United States and abroad. See, for example, *Learning for Careers: The Pathways to Prosperity Network* (2017) and *Vocational Education and Training for a Global Economy: Lessons from Four Countries* (2019).[2] Hence, it is worth a word about an early book in the Work and Learning Series entitled *Youth, Education, and the Role of Society* by Robert Halpern.[3]

Beginning with articles in the 2000s and culminating in this 2013 HEP book, Halpern argued that schools don't just bore many young people; they actually impede young people from growing up. Just as adolescents are beginning to think seriously about what their adult lives will be like and what they want to be out in the world testing their adult futures, schools keep them segregated with their same age peers. As Halpern concludes, "The very type of experiences that young people most need are the hardest to come by in American culture.... Key social institutions misread what autonomy and choice mean when it comes to young people, or they let these constructs serve as excuses for keeping them at the margins of the adult world." That book with its mundane title made Halpern a prophet in his time.[4]

While from John Dewey on, hands-on or experiential learning has characterized progressive learning theory, only in the last several decades, spurred by much too slow progress on equity of outcomes, has a new version of career-focused education come to the fore exemplifying today's approach to hands-on learning to prepare for the new realities of work. Halpern's was an early voice advocating for what has become the current wave of interest in vocational education. He thought vocational education unfairly stigmatized when it—not "narrow academic learning"—was the best preparation for "the changing nature of work." In his book, he laments how little schools help young people even "tentatively confirm and disconfirm vocational interests." He goes on to note, "Whether or not they enjoy it, young people know the social role of student. Most young people know far less about what it means to be a worker—the nature and structure of tasks, the daily rhythm, the dynamics of workplace relationships—and most know little or nothing about what it means to work in a particular vocational field." They get little help developing what Halpern calls "a guiding vocational narrative."[5]

Even in 2018, when the Gates Foundation funded *Striving to Thriving: Occupational Identity Formation among Black and Hispanic Young People and Young People from Households with Lower Incomes*, the massive research project that inspired *How We See Us*, a commissioned background paper declared that "occupational identity development is an underexplored piece of the puzzle in improving pathways to occupations for youth, and particularly important when they are from underrepresented groups."[6] It is this theme—how adolescents and emerging adults are supported and enabled to explore and build a vocational identity—that ties Halpern's work and Leslie-Rule's together.

While the field has come a long way in destigmatizing vocational education (called career and technical education today) over the last ten years and career-focused high school education has become acceptable for all students, clearly many young people who speak up in *How We See Us* are still constructing a "guiding vocational narrative" absent the experiences and supports that adults and institutions could do a better job providing. But institutions and mentors can't do it all. One takeaway particularly has influenced me and the work of the Jobs for the Future (JFF) team to improve how we design career pathways. We are moving to more systematically include what studies like Halpern's and Leslie-Rule's have taught us. The young people interviewed—just like older people, just like us—put finding a vocation in a broader context. Yes, careers matter, but asked by the moderator at the end of a session what the conversation was about, Cedric says: "It was about life" (page 82). And that's something for us to remember.

Preface

A DEATH IN THE FAMILY

When I was fifteen, I recorded my grandfather's story as he neared death. We sat in the upstairs bedroom of the house on Romaine Place, where my mother and her sisters grew up. I remember the room had 1970s décor, including plush carpet and a vanity where my grandmother used to smoke and paint her nails red. I remember noticing how my grandfather's legs seemed to reach over the side of the bed, his slippered feet hanging inches from the floor, and how his robe and pajamas hung from his emaciated frame when he stood. I remember struggling to reconcile how this person, with his bones on display, could be the same man who baked butter cakes and peach cobblers, watched WWF religiously, and whose laugh could fill the whole house. My mother had tried to prepare me for this. She'd said that it would be normal to feel scared—and I was. I remember he seemed so small and so impermanent.

In Seattle, my mom worked at a public television station. Her job came with some perks for me. Most importantly the opportunity to experiment with video storytelling and ultimately bring a Hi-8 camera with me to St. Louis. This was Christmas, a year before I would decide to do the Running Start program, a dual-enrollment option at my high school and a local community college, graduate a year early, and move to New York to attend college.

My mom and I had discussed the idea of recording the family story from my grandfather's perspective. I am almost ten years older than my nearest first cousin, so while I remember my grandfather, they do not. Perhaps she thought this would be a gift to them. Perhaps it was an attempt to lift my grandfather's spirits—giving him a much-needed chuckle, seeing the seriousness with which I approached the conversation. Perhaps it was her typically good and advanced planning—knowing that she would be occupied with the adult business of preparing for the death of a family member and that I would be bored and alone in a house bursting with too much silence and so much grief.

Whatever the genesis of the moment, I felt purpose in the task. I remember feeling a deep responsibility in the moments leading up to our chat—maybe even a feeling of loneliness that crept in when I understood the singularity of the opportunity. I was fifteen, and he wasn't even seventy. I asked him what it was like to grow up in rural Mississippi, what he remembered of the grandfather who raised him, and what he would have liked to become had our country been better to Black men and to poor men at that time. I remember asking him what he hoped and dreamt of for us, his descendants.

Sitting across from my grandfather in that room was the first time, in what would become a long practice, that I intentionally constructed a space where I invited someone else to speak about their life and experiences and elevated their voice above my own. Admittedly, at fifteen, the stories my grandfather told me may have been a little more sanitized than they would have been had I been older or perhaps male. But even so, the experience sparked a deep curiosity about other people—how they see themselves, create and understand the worlds around them, what they believe they can control, and what they know they cannot. It wasn't the recording of the story or watching it that felt important to me. It was the living of it, the experience of listening to and memorializing the story, that mattered. It was the practice of writing down my questions for him, how my legs felt sitting on the bed and then the chair across from him, viewing him in double—once through the viewfinder and once unencumbered with my naked eye. It was the *being* with him even as so little of his physical body remained, even when he was so clearly and painfully leaving. I haven't watched that video in years—maybe twenty. But looking back, I know that his voice, laughter, slight shifts in his chair, and even his silence changed how I saw the world and my role in it. I can only hope that he was made more comfortable and ready to make his transition, knowing his story was safe with me. I hope that telling his story changed something in him, too.

LISTENING WITH INTENTION

When I was nineteen, I moved to Cape Town, South Africa. I remember the night before I left: I had stayed up all night packing—with the help of my childhood best friend—a ridiculously tall, blue-and-black backpack in my parent's basement. My aunt, who had lived and worked in South Africa during the apartheid era, poked fun at me when she saw the bag (and my rolls of toilet paper and ziplocked tampons) and asked me, "Where do you think you are going?"

It was 1997 when I arrived in Cape Town; three years since the first democratic election and the ascendance of Nelson Mandela, the first Black South African elected to that nation's presidential office.

My study abroad classmates and I were typically and pathetically underprepared, unskilled students with an almost ridiculous amount of *unearned* access to people who were in the process of building a new and unprecedented multiracial democracy. The country felt open and full of possibility. We walked into the parliament building, sat in on several sessions of the Truth and Reconciliation Commission proceedings, and had internships in the offices of Archbishop Desmond Tutu. Being outside the United States gave me the space and perspective to become deeply curious about my life, identity, and experiences of Blackness. I could reflect for the first time on my family's expectations for my life and how these expectations resulted in a nearly myopic understanding of how achievement and success looked and felt. Later, this clarity about myself would push me to interrogate the nearly ubiquitous narratives about Black people to which I'd been exposed growing up in the United States: in particular those that centered around Black death and Black struggle. I felt that by focusing on our stories—those that we tell ourselves about ourselves, and that provide the nuance and meaning behind our experiences of life and Blackness—I could center Black life.

While in South Africa, I lived in Gugulethu, a Black township in Western Cape located about twenty kilometers outside of Cape Town. At a local university, my coursework included classes on the impact of art and creative practice in the fight against apartheid. Six months into my stay, I auditioned for and was accepted to an apprenticeship with one of the most storied dance companies in the country. The multiracial ensemble had been integrated during the 1980s, one of the most fraught decades in the apartheid era, and would become the first and, for many years, the only company of its kind in the country. It was in the rehearsal studios, in the canteen, and on the minibus taxis to and from Gugulethu, and later the Cape Town neighborhood of Observatory, where I came face-to-face with my privilege, meeting young people my age who had spent their childhoods fighting for the right of self-determination and freedom and against the evils of colonialism and white supremacy. I struggled to make sense of my own experiences when those of my peers felt so much more serious and meaningful than my own.

My time in South Africa culminated with a capstone project. Growing up, my mother's long-term partner had been a social worker at the height of the AIDS epidemic. I'd spent much of middle and high school visiting young gay men dying brutal deaths in hospice care, and participating in protests urging U.S. presidents George H. W. Bush and Bill Clinton to commit more resources to developing a cure. In Gugulethu, HIV/AIDS was ravaging whole communities. I chose to interview and record young mothers who had contracted HIV/AIDS, in part because I felt the other dimensions of their lives, their dreams, ideas, and families had been overshadowed by their diagnosis and illness. This was several years before South Africa would have widespread access to anti-retroviral medications (ARVs), a lifesaving combination of drugs that would transform the lives of people living with HIV. In the late nineties, many women, showing signs of infection, were pushed out of their family homes and communities and others were abandoned by men who had impregnated them. If they were lucky, they found shelter and later hospice care where they could be made comfortable, or at least warm, until they died. I began spending time at a shelter run by Catholic nuns who fed and cared for HIV-positive women and their young children, who were often also positive. Three women permitted me to interview them and record messages from them to their children, and, in doing so, we co-created a tangible artifact for them to leave behind.

Perched on the edge of beds covered in worn and sometimes tattered sheets, I recorded hours of stories and memories—the day a child was born, the day a young woman learned they were pregnant, their wishes and desires for their children, their hopes for how the world might change. Sometimes, I would sit with the children in the crèche—the childcare attached to the hospice—play with them and tell them stories about my own home and family. With the women's permission, I anonymized the recordings to share them more broadly with local leaders and policymakers advocating for increased resources for children and families affected by the disease. And here again, I felt the profound responsibility of holding stories for safekeeping.

In my early twenties and thirties, I led a writing and performance workshop in a state prison where women and girls were incarcerated. Participants in the workshop recorded stories about their childhood memories. Families and friends outside the prison received these recordings and responded with other stories. Together, these storytellers, inside and outside of the prison walls, built collaborative recollections of the women's youth and life before incarceration: an artifact for the families missing them and the women themselves.

Over the past twenty years, I have been many things: a theater-maker, a teaching artist, a campaigner, an organizer, a researcher, and a cultural strategist. Throughout all of this, it is the act of constructing space for people to talk about how they see themselves and the world that remains constant. It is the stories that remain the most precious and the most powerful tool for transformational change.

I hold this belief, despite being told more times than I can count, that stories are nice, but quantitative data is king. After all, our governments, philanthropic institutions, legislative leaders, and policymakers often exclusively define impact in quantifiable terms (i.e., bar charts and percentages). Quantitative data is prized for its supposed objectivity and generalizability, while qualitative data is considered soft, subjective, and anecdotal.

But bar charts and percentages rarely change hearts and minds. As human beings, it is our stories that shift our attitudes and mindsets and enable us to see the possibilities for radical change. Stories offer us the language, frames, and metaphors we need to understand the world around us in new and interesting ways. They allow us to consider the world through someone else's eyes and empathize with their experiences and their choices. They teach us ways of seeing and they change us; as listeners and storytellers.

In the twenty years that I have made listening part of my practice, I've come to believe that stories teach us something else, too: they teach us about hope. Through stories, we can learn how hope is inherited, created, nurtured, and understood by people who take vastly different paths in life.

There was hope in the listening. I listened expectantly, hoping I had created the space and time that each storyteller deserved to speak their truth about the path they'd traveled. And even in the briefest of these encounters, I was affected and moved in ways that, even here, I find hard to articulate. Perhaps there was hope in the telling of the story, too. Perhaps my grandfather's spirit felt a little lighter as he sat with me that day and recounted his childhood in Mississippi, knowing that I would have his story with me always. Perhaps the mothers in Gugulethu found some hope knowing that their children would know something more about them long after they themselves had passed on.

As I travel my own career path, I will continue to be an evangelist for stories—showing others how sharing stories can change us all for the better. Having that belief affirmed and reaffirmed is one of the main forces that brought me to this book, and the opportunity to write about a period of time I spent listening to young people in focus groups and interviews exploring how they formed identities as learners and workers and how they imagined their future lives. Many of the significant insights from the research project *Striving to Thriving* have been written about and shared, and I'll reference some of them throughout the book.[1] However, this book is a collection of young people's stories—the experiences that led to the insights—and an invitation to consider how telling and listening to these stories changed them and me, and ultimately, I hope, might change you.

INTRODUCTION

The "Why" and the "What" of This Book

Now, let's get into what brought me to write this book specifically. Over the last two decades, I have probably read variations of the phrase "Black people are in *crisis*" several thousand times. In a Google search in early 2022, if I substituted *Black students* for *Black people* and searched for articles related to education, the results included headlines that addressed racism, trauma, mental health, and learning loss during the pandemic. These articles often feature quotes that include a series of well-worn euphemisms used mostly to describe children of color: vulnerable, at risk, marginalized, traumatized, and so on. The intended meaning of these words is clear: we, Black people, and our children are suffering. Done again, this time replacing *Black students* with *Hispanic students* the search revealed an abundance of disparity measures: less likely to graduate from high school, less likely to enroll in college after graduating from high school, less likely to graduate from college, more likely to earn significantly less than white peers once employed.

The exact crises from which these young people suffer change over time, but the underlying narrative (or belief) seems to persist. And it is this: Black and Hispanic young people are living in communities, families, and geographies from which they must be rescued. Another widely held belief further cements this crisis narrative in our collective imagination (even though much research suggests the opposite);[1] that young people, particularly those who are Black and Hispanic and young people who come from lower-income communities, lack the confidence, life experience, motivation, and resilience to exercise agency in their own lives. These narratives stigmatize and problematize young people, their families, and their communities. At the same time, the narratives normalize the perception that all valuable knowledge and meaningful interventions are created outside of Black and Hispanic communities by primarily white institutions and affluent adults.

As I said at the outset, the power of stories is something I've lived and breathed for most of my life. But it is only in the last decade or so that I began to write and think more specifically about how narratives are constructed and, increasingly, how they can be disrupted.

While a story is often powerful because it is singular and unique, narratives, evident across a collection of stories, are powerful because they are repeated across many stories. As narratives become embedded into popular culture, government, and philanthropy, and repeated in our homes and communities, they become shared beliefs about how the world works. Narratives are the themes and ideas carried in a collection of stories that uphold a particular frame or worldview.[2] If stories are tiles, narratives are the mosaic.[3]

The same collection of stories can carry several narratives. Some narratives may appear helpful, and others harmful. In the Comic Book canon, a fictional example I often use, stories about superheroes Batman, Spiderman, and Superman convey narratives about the importance of using one's power to help others. At the same time, these superhero stories carry more potentially harmful narratives about the lack of agency of everyday people.

When the dominant group in a society creates and amplifies patterns of stories (mosaics) that reinforce the group's power and uphold the status quo, they are what Rashad Robinson calls "dominant narratives."[4] Many "dominant narratives" about Black and Brown young people not only obscure the rich diversity of their experiences but also lock them into narratives of crisis. Here it feels important to recognize that sometimes crisis narratives are constructed intentionally by people like me, who specialize in creating narrative change strategies. For example, my colleagues and I often wield crisis narratives in education and health care to mobilize our fellow citizens to address disparities and confront societal inequities by voting. Used in these ways, our narratives may try to remind would-be voters of the stakes of their vote or the cost of their silence: the impact of their actions. However, despite these good intentions, narratives of crisis often reinforce the very beliefs that we seek to subvert or change. This can happen in a variety of ways.

In the case of education, a crisis narrative draws power by focusing on what can be done by teachers, students, and families to address the racial and economic achievement gap, instead of focusing on the broken systems and structures that perpetuate long-standing racial and economic inequities. As a society, we are fascinated by stories about young people, particularly a Black or Hispanic young person, who "beat the odds," completing their education through hard work and grit, and succeeding in their career aspirations. Underpinning these stories are dominant narratives about the role of education as the great equalizer (i.e., if only you get an education, all will be well in your life), and the importance of pulling yourself up by your bootstraps (i.e., nothing worth doing is easy, the most valuable achievements are those accomplished alone). Dominant narratives about education place the burden of building and navigating education pathways on the students themselves, minimizing in our collective imagination how systems impact and shape students' learning environments (e.g., which schools have more or less funding, frequency of testing, and assessment). These systems often propagate and perpetuate the racial and gender inequities that so often get in the way of students' dreams.[5]

Narratives about "beating the odds" through individual effort and perseverance influence our understanding of fairness, determining who deserves help, and when. Importantly, these narratives connect to our sense of possibility: while some students can overcome obstacles, others cannot. Of course, the truth is far more complicated than that, but as my brilliant colleague and friend Zakiya Harris often says, "The currency of narrative is not truth; it is meaning."

First, these narratives about education are powerful. They reinforce the dominant group's worldview and validate their experiences: in this case, that those who succeed deserve to succeed, and that navigating the very same systems that entrap and derail many students of color is a matter of effort and not resources or luck.

Second, a crisis narrative requires a clear distinction between an "Us" and a "Them." "Us" consists of those who can help. "Them" is made up of those who need help. Typically, "Us" is imbued with greater nuance. When "Them" is described, the richness of individual experiences is flattened to focus only on whatever deficit or need we perceive there to be. In describing "Us," individual stories are seen to be of value, so *our* differences and similarities are described more richly. In the case of education, the "Us" can be affluent parents of primarily white children who themselves sought or were expected to pursue higher education. The "Us" is sometimes also those who feel they once were in need but have somehow left that life and those experiences and are now—often due to education and wealth—driven to help. "Us," because we perceive our differences as valuable and worthy of being considered, is deserving of bespoke programs and interventions. We and our children deserve to be seen as *both* individuals and group members. In contrast, "Them" is the young people on whose behalf "Us" must work and build solutions. "Them" is often described as a monolithic category devoid of meaningful diversity—"Them" are reduced to their Blackness, their Brownness, their low income, and the connection of these characteristics to predetermined measures of success.

Third, to be deemed worthy of intervention, our crisis narratives have the effect of requiring young people of color and young people from lower-income communities to *remain* in a state of crisis. Crisis narratives imbue our work with a sense of urgency and provide us with a perennial North Star for our work, building solutions and advancing equity. If the story we tell ourselves is that we are helpers, then Black and Hispanic students must continue to require our help.

Every day, we are exposed to narratives that tell us what power looks like, what problems are worthy of solving, and who can and should develop solutions. While the human brain may be hardwired to put things and people into categories, narratives help us to assign meaning to those categories. Our narratives make it easier to believe that being Black, Hispanic, or poor supersedes every other aspect of young people's identities, making these characteristics the most important lens through which we can understand these young people's education and early career experiences.

Categorization is not without merit. It has its place. Broad categories allow us to see patterns and themes, articulate insights, and ultimately create the kinds of generalizable knowledge that are often leveraged to advance systemic change. However, our system of categorization has limitations because it distances us from young people's lived experiences and, therefore, their individual stories. Our shorthand use of labels and categories effectively erases or provides very little space for the diversity of young people's voices. We design interventions aimed at impacting young people's education and career goals in response to outcomes data, disaggregated by race and gender, but not on young people's actual lives. In fact, young people's ideas, experiences, perspectives, and unique intelligences are deemed less credible by adults than those of the adults themselves. The voices of Black, Hispanic, and young people from lower-income backgrounds are even further undervalued. In an environment of institutional racism, xenophobia, classism, and other biases, these young people are often incorrectly perceived as being less knowledgeable and having less agency in their own lives than their white and more affluent peers.[6]

Why does this happen? In short, engaging with young people as individuals is more difficult than summarizing data that portrays young people in monolithic categories. We can see this tension between the general and the specific in research that philanthropy initiates, the interventions that program designers create, and how we assign value to specific types of knowledge. Even if we have the opportunity to see and hear young people's individual stories, it is difficult to resist the urge to translate each story into an existing broader narrative—often a narrative of convenience—about a group of people. For example, in the research project at the heart of this book, we asked young people how they would describe their racial and ethnic backgrounds. We learned that young people use the term "Hispanic" more than other words, such as Latino or Latinx, to describe themselves and their racial and ethnic identities. This is consistent with a Pew Research finding in 2020 that the majority of adults of Latin American descent prefer the term Hispanic.[7] However, I must admit to feeling some pressure to use the term Latinx in this book—a term used by many of my peers—despite knowing that this is not a term used by the young people with whom we spoke.

In our rush to show scale and to make larger and salient points, even those of us with the most training and the best intentions sometimes forfeit the opportunity to engage with the complexities of individual lives and, specifically, the nuanced voices of youth. Generalizable knowledge is the gold standard and within that frame, young people's voices often cannot be anything more than anecdotal inputs to more reducible insights.

This absence of youth voices can have profound consequences. Our general understanding of Black and Hispanic young people's experiences leads to similarly general interventions. We build approaches based not on lived experiences but instead on group-level insights—the kind that can credibly serve as an evidence base to justify broader strategies, be it policy, grantmaking, communications, programs, or something else. But when young people's experiences, aspirations, and goals are not adequately taken into consideration, adults are more likely to produce tools and services that inadequately support young people's ability to attain their future goals. Adults are also more likely to create and amplify narratives that perpetuate the belief that something is wrong with poor young people and young people of color.

This devaluation of young people's experiences is not malicious. We do this, in part, because our projects rarely have the resources or the vision to adequately include young people as stakeholders, decision-makers, and co-creators. We ask organizations serving young people to act as a proxy, bending to fit themselves and the young people with whom they work into preset categories to match our preset understanding of how problems are defined, and to fit within parameters of "viable" solutions. One group, serving as a proxy, defines the challenges and opportunities for the other groups—young people of color and young people who come from lower-income families. Their voices, and agency, are often lost or obscured.

If the quality of our solutions depends on how richly we draw the problem, then we as researchers, program designers, educators, and policy makers, need to better understand how young people who are Black and Hispanic and lower-income are experiencing and navigating the journey from youth to adulthood—how they are traveling toward their career aspirations and their future goals.[8] We need to infuse our narratives with the lived experiences and the language of young people who have the most at stake. We need to ask ourselves how we can create and hold space for these young people to meaningfully contribute to and direct our work. We need to question why we so readily tailor interventions for affluent young people and provide off-the-shelf interventions for young people from lower-income communities. We must get better at not only amplifying youth voices but also centering their expertise and their knowledge so that we can become more accountable to who they are and who they aspire to be. In short, we must get closer to young people and their experiences, and we must get better at listening.

A RESEARCH DESIGN THAT PRIVILEGES YOUTH VOICE

In the summer of 2018, my colleagues and I set out to build a research project that would explicitly center Black and Hispanic young people and young people from lower-income communities. The research population included Black and Hispanic young people of all incomes and white young people from lower-income households. The research sought to understand these young people's lived experiences, emotions, and beliefs and how they developed their occupational identities—that is, how they see their future selves in the workplace, what they like to do, what skills they believe they have, and where they feel they belong.[9]

The Heartwired methodology, on which this research is based, centers discourse and narrative.[10] The methodology, developed by Amy Simon and Robert Pérez, is an approach to audience research and values-based messaging that builds on neurological and psychosocial research; it explains how humans process emotion and logic, and how these processes influence our decisions, attitudes, and behaviors. The experimental design of this book draws on Heartwired and the academic literature around narrative and storytelling. Specifically, I utilize psychological and sociological theories that suggest narrative immersion and narrative transportation are unique features of storytelling and create opportunities for increased intimacy and proximity to novel concepts, enabling more proactive engagement and empathy with new people and ideas.[11]

In its design, the research project recognized and deferred to these young people as the de facto experts on their own life experiences and, therefore, the people most equipped to tell field experts how they see themselves and how they relate to and envision the paths that will lead them to their future lives. Entitled *Striving to Thriving*, the project aimed to better understand how young people think about and navigate paths toward education and careers.[12] Rather than relying on adult proxies to situate young people's experiences within our existing frameworks and agendas, *Striving to Thriving* spoke with young people directly. The researchers then used young people's words, phrases, and metaphors as the preliminary themes for analysis and, ultimately, the foundation for its frameworks. Between November 2018 and June 2019, a research team led by Amy Simon, the founder and principal of Goodwin Simon Strategic Research, and I conducted forty-two focus groups with Black, Hispanic, and white young people aged fifteen to twenty-one across the United States (a full methodology is available in Appendix A, at the end of this book). We conducted additional research with parents, guardians, and adult influencers of young people in the aforementioned age groups. My colleagues and I used a mixed-method research design that included in-person and online focus groups, in-depth interviews, and a national online survey. Each focus group was comprised of young people who self-identified as the same race and gender. The groups and in-depth interviews were conducted by professional moderators who matched the race or ethnicity of the group. We find that participants often feel more comfortable talking about race and ethnicity when everyone in the group is perceived as sharing their racial or ethnic identity. Subverting the norm, we conducted our qualitative research and then used the online survey to validate what we'd seen and observed at scale. Our qualitative research used a conversational structure that privileged youth voices above that of the adult moderator. This enabled youth participants to exert more control over the direction of the conversation and to speak about their life experiences, dreams, and future aspirations without fear of adult judgment (or interjection). We wanted to understand:

- What does meaningful employment for a happy, productive life look like through the eyes of young people?
- Who are the people, and what are the resources, that help them along the way?
- What barriers do they experience that limit or divert them on the way to success?
- How do they understand their identities in relation to education and career?
- What do they feel they are good at?

After the project concluded in 2020, we did everything that one usually does when wrapping up a massive research project—we disseminated the research. We built a website. We used the findings as leverage to propose and conduct other projects centering young people's experiences, for instance, a youth survey to understand how young people were faring during the COVID-19 pandemic.

We attended conferences and facilitated workshops, sharing what we learned from our focus groups, interviews, and surveys. While we spent a great deal of time talking about the research insights related to occupational identity, I realize now that we spent far too little time reflecting on and articulating the unintended impacts of the focus groups for the young people themselves.[13] Young people who participated in the focus groups found value in the conversations, and this altered the focus groups from a purely extractive experience into one that felt more mutually beneficial. In session after session, we saw young people attach value to the research tools that extended beyond the conversation they were having in the room and toward their everyday lives; we also saw young people lift one another up, confide in one another, and offer to be a support to one another in the future. For example, several participants took photographs of an exercise they completed during the focus groups to remind them of what they had uncovered or articulated about their future career pathways during the discussion (see chapter 4 about the unintended and positive impacts of the research model on participants).

We watched young people work through their own questions of what it meant to be capable of changing and directing one's own life. They grappled with their expectations for themselves and those held for them by adults in their lives. They formed a deeper understanding of the pathways to work and careers that lay ahead of them and the steps they hoped would take them to their version of a good life. In conversation with their peers, their own struggles and fears were validated. The groups functioned as an affirmation of sorts.

THE POWER OF YOUTH VOICE

To write that young people's voices are important is not a particularly radical statement. A fascination with and acknowledgment of youth culture is nearly ubiquitous in our daily lives. Everyone, from social media influencers and advertisers to political strategists, seeks to leverage the ingenuity, wit, creativity, optimism, and imagination of young people. In the nonprofit and social sectors, *voice* has become a rallying cry—a value-laden proclamation brandished by policymakers, grantmakers, and solutions builders—to communicate that they are both in touch with and listening to their constituents.

Most of this is purely performative. Most adults have very limited interactions with young people. If we are not educators or providers of direct services of which young people are the primary consumers or beneficiaries, most adults' interactions with young people are often limited to our own children, the children of our friends, and perhaps the young people in our immediate communities. From this, we extrapolate. For an example of this, consider the generalizations made about millennials, or members of Gen Z. Our conversations or interactions with a small group of young people inform our sense of who young people are as a generation, how they are experiencing the world, what aspirations they hold for their own lives, and what steps toward those aspirations can and should look like.

Based on this small sample size, we may believe that young people are capable, resourceful, optimistic, and full of agency, or we may believe that young people are ill-equipped and uninformed, unable to make decisions, or subjects that need to be acted upon. We have a problem of scale. Without an evidence base that describes life experiences, identities, geographies, and education pathways different from our own, we can continue to assume that the young people we happen to know best are representative of youth as a whole. In the United States, where our lives become increasingly segregated by race, education, income, neighborhood, and school, opportunities to immerse ourselves in the stories of people whose experiences differ from our own are few and far between.

An argument for immersion

In strategic communications, it doesn't matter whether a narrative is factually inconsistent or false. It matters whether people believe it is true. So how do we counter perceptions of what is true about young people of color and young people from households with lower incomes? Proximity. When we immerse ourselves in young people's words and ideas, we become directly engaged with youth. We hear and feel how young people understand their emerging identities, and we see how they experience and assign meaning to events along their education journeys. As we listen, our perception of the world—what knowledge is valuable, what problems need to be solved and by whom, what success looks like, and how adults can show up in young people's lives—risks changing. And it's true; we adults don't always have the time, resources, or appetite for change.[14]

This book seeks to bring educators, policymakers, researchers, and other adults working to make our systems and institutions more equitable into closer proximity with young people. I invite readers to immerse themselves, as I have, in the voices of young people whose stories informed the *Striving to Thriving* research. I urge readers to consider what they can do to more authentically and intentionally center a greater diversity of young people's voices in their work.

This book is also an experiment. Earlier, I wrote that the *Striving to Thriving* research design aimed to subvert some long-held traditions, wherein adult influencers—teachers, parents, or other adults—act as a proxy for young people's voices. While our design succeeded in some respects, I feel our report failed to fully disrupt these norms. Young people's voices were presented anecdotally in our report—often a series of short quotes contextualized by the researchers' analysis and framing. The presentation of the research findings in this way required individual young people's stories and voices to be shared in service of common themes and generalizable statements.

Readers of the report were not immersed in young people's voices so much as haltingly introduced to a series of quotes presented as evidence of whatever finding was explained in the paragraphs before or after. As I reflected on this, I wondered what it might look like to center young people's voices—not only in creating knowledge but also in disseminating and discussing that knowledge.

To explore this, I've made choices about the narrative structure and the sequence in which I introduce the research participants and the group discussions. Instead of short quotes, I have included longer sections from the transcripts, thereby sharing a fuller and more accurate depiction of how each conversation unfolded. In doing so, I want to enable the reader to listen more closely, reading and hearing youth research participants as full and multidimensional people.

I have also chosen to write about and, therefore, to focus your attention on the voices of Black and Hispanic young people in particular. I do this for two reasons: 1) If one way of countering problematic and harmful narratives about Black and Hispanic young people is to introduce new stories into our collective consciousness that counter or complicate the existing narratives—it is my obligation to do so; 2) I have a unique perspective on the importance of *Striving to Thriving* for adults working with and for Black youth. In addition to serving as a lead researcher across the project, I moderated the focus groups and interviews with Black research participants. I was most proximate to their voices and experiences throughout the project.

The structure of the book provides three different levels at which we can listen to young people's experiences, perceptions, and expectations of education and work. First, in chapter 1, through a series of short vignettes, we meet four young people growing up and making sense of their experiences and the world in dramatically different parts of the United States: Greenville, Mississippi; Oakland, California; Belle Glade, Florida; and New York, New York. Their names and personal identifiers have been changed to protect the anonymity of the participants. The vignettes allow us to hear one young person's voice clearly—zooming in on their individual voice and story by removing the voices of the other focus group participants. At the tail end of this chapter, I provide some landmarks—an introduction to a metaphor for how young people think about and experience work: surviving, striving, and thriving. Then, we listen to young people as members of a group. In chapter 2, we listen to eight young Black men in New York City as they describe their experiences and expectations of jobs, work, and career. And in chapter 3, the steps, stages, experiences, and support the young Black men in New York feel they will need to move from where they are now to the lives they imagine for themselves. Here, we will revisit the surviving, striving, and thriving metaphor, and using the image of a pathway as an anchor, hear and see young people's mindsets, aspirations, and expectations as they navigate their education and career journeys, and the barriers they imagine might get in the way of their goals. In chapter 4 we shift gears and explore the unintended impacts of the focus group methodology on the youth participants and on me, as a moderator. Then in chapter 5, I share guidance for how you can use these frameworks and insights from the research to transform your own work and develop or improve your own listening practice. Chapter 5 is followed by two appendices. The first details the research methodology in its entirety, including an example focus group moderator's guide, and the second provides suggestions for how to use a pathway mapping exercise in ways that encourage students to think about and plan for their futures.

Read from cover to cover, this book intends to provide a counter to the narratives of crises Black and Hispanic young people, in particular, are forced to endure.

In thinking about a title for this book, I was inspired by the Ava Duvernay film *When They See Us*, which heartbreakingly depicts how the white gaze brutally and irreparably changed the lives of five Black teen boys in New York. By foregrounding the narratives that young people, in particular Black and Hispanic young people hold for and about themselves, the book offers a vision of young people *as they see themselves*, not solely as how *we as adults see them*. In a sense, within the pages of the book, young people become the "we," the ones whose gaze is valued and whose perspective and knowledge the reader is asked to consider. *How We See Us* aims, if only briefly, to allow young people the space, and pages, to be authors of their own stories.

It is my hope that my and my colleagues' success in engaging young people in authentic conversation about their lives and career goals can be useful to those of you who are committed to partnering with young people as they build pathways to their imagined futures.

CHAPTER 1

Vignettes: Young People, Uninterrupted

When I transitioned from being a listener and interpreter of research with young people to being the author of this book, I had to confront, head-on, a fundamental problem that is present in much of the work and thought leadership about how best to support young people. Many adults, with the best intentions, have professionalized the support of and care for young people, yet the work is missing the voices and perspectives of young people themselves.

As my colleagues and I traveled the country to present our research findings, we attended conferences and led workshops and webinars focused on K–12 education and workforce development. As time passed, I grew increasingly uncomfortable with these presentations because they began feeling abstract and distant from the young people who had trusted us with their stories. Moreover, we saw few, if any, young people in the room. Young people, the most important participants in and beneficiaries of our education system—indeed, the entire reason our education system exists—were relegated to mere pawns, subjects of a machine built and perpetuated by adults.

So, in writing this book, I sought to find the right tone, format, and style to immerse audiences in Black and Hispanic young people's words, ideas, and perspectives because this type of immersion will enable more adults to see and feel the fullness and richness of these young people's lives. Building greater proximity to young people's experiences and imagined futures can engender greater accountability and a deeper commitment to change the policies and systems that are too often barriers to their success. At the same time, I hoped to inspire a practice of listening more deeply to young people and centering their experiences in projects, approaches and interventions developed on their behalf. A report is an imperfect vehicle for this—not only because of the volume of the findings but also because of the constraints of the report structure and format.

As I wrote in the introduction, I chose to write this book in part to subvert some of the norms of how researchers share knowledge and, in particular, how the format and style in which we share young people's voices implicitly reinforces the notion that knowledge held by young people is somehow lesser than that held by the adults who study and write about them. In a report, young people's voices are presented almost anecdotally. Often, they appear as a series of quotes contextualized by the researchers' analysis and framing. Presenting research findings this way requires that individual young people's stories and voices be in service of common themes and generalizable statements.

This book allows me to do something I've been unable to do in presentations thus far. Here, I can share more in-depth stories from some of the young people who shared their lives and dreams with us by presenting their words and ideas as fully as possible and not as brief quotes to support a set of findings.

Why do I think it's important to do this? Because I am sure that the further we get into our adult years, the more we begin to assume too much about young people's experiences, and, perhaps more importantly, we assume too much about the *meaning* that young people derive from their experiences. We believe young people are in crisis and thus we must act quickly, or else young people will be lost to us. While it may be admirable to act with urgency when thinking about the best ways to support young people, we still need to remember to address not only the barriers as we perceive them but also the barriers (and opportunities) as young people themselves experience them.

I like to imagine that many of us—educators, program designers, policymakers, and strategists—are inspired, in part, to do the work of making education better because of our own experiences with or as young people. Yet once we become the designers of policies and programs, we may feel compelled to create interventions that service an impersonal aggregate. Yes, anything we build or develop to help young people navigate the transition to adulthood should support the young people that research has shown suffer the worst educational and economic outcomes. But what we build should include and not limit the ongoing opportunity to see young people as individuals with stories and aspirations of their own that are important—in fact, central—in shaping their future lives.

This chapter features the voices of and stories from four young people: two Black and two Hispanic. I selected these particular participants, in part, because they forced me to listen differently. These young people are not telling us simple stories that lead us to neat and uncomplicated solutions. They are instead telling us about several dimensions of what it means to be young and to make decisions in pursuit of their goals and aspirations. Some have a firm grasp of both a goal and what they may need to get there, and others have a more tenuous grip on all that lies ahead.

As you read, you may be tempted to focus on the aspects of young people's experiences that most align with whatever intervention or program with which you are most familiar. This is the way we are taught to read young people's stories—as if their words are proof points confirming truths we have already defined. This interpretation of young people's stories easily dismisses their agency and their self-efficacy, in service of your own.[1] I urge you, instead, to consider each speaker's voice: the many ways in which they are examining and experiencing the tensions in their own lives, the ways in which they assign meaning to the challenges they face, and, perhaps most importantly, what their vision is for themselves and their own imagining of the good life they would one day like to experience.[2]

My goal is to give you the proximity to young people's voices and stories that is so often missing from our work—especially at scale when we are by definition solving for population-level wrongs. The chapter is constructed around a series of vignettes. Each one tells the story of a single young person. Try to let their voice come alive on the page, let their ideas play out, and limit or perhaps at least remain aware of your own desire to interject.

While I've tried to present the original quotes as young people said them, I also appreciate the risk of sharing them without any framing or commentary whatsoever. Without the benefit of actually being in these rooms and hearing and observing the interaction with the other participants in the groups, some of these excerpts might seem opaque. When I think it will assist in communicating the meaning or intention behind a statement, I have also included some additional context-setting that enables you to better understand what was happening in the room or how the other participants responded to what the speaker said or discussed. In each vignette, *italicized text* represents verbatims taken from the transcript of the focus group and reprinted here; **bold text** is used to denote the places in which I share my own observations or helpful context from the other participants in the group. In some instances, I have also included the worksheet or moderator's prompt to provide additional context in bracketed plain text. My intention has been to restrain my own adult voice to leave you with plenty of room to insert your own interpretations and reactions. As you read, you might consider the following questions:

- How are these young people planning for their futures? Who among them feels they are only just starting out, and who feels they are well on their way?
- What support do these young people have, and what do they feel they need?
- What dreams does each young person hold for themselves?

Meaning-making is unique. In your efforts to listen to these young people and hear what they're saying, other useful questions might emerge. If you find yourself identifying themes or patterns of insights to make meaning of what you are reading, you may want to take notes. I encourage you not to let yourself be distracted by your own voice, or your own knowledge and expertise. At the end of this chapter, I'll share some of the ways in which my colleagues and I framed and made sense of our observations.

In addition to the *words* of each young person, each participant was encouraged to complete a visual "pathway", an image they filled out in the course of the group conversations. Each drew, wrote, and colored the image to reflect where they were; where they wanted to be; and the steps, stages, experiences, and people they may need to draw on to get there. They were also asked to write down what, or who, they thought would help them reach their goal and who, or what, might stand in their way.

Each young person treated the image as a map—a visual record of the conversation. The resulting images—some written in brightly colored ink (but presented in black and white in the pages that follow), some with doodles in the margins, some steps shaded in, and others written only in blue or black ink—showed us something personal about themselves and how they envisioned their future lives; but it also prompted the participants to engage in the creation and

FIGURE 1.1   Blank Pathway Image

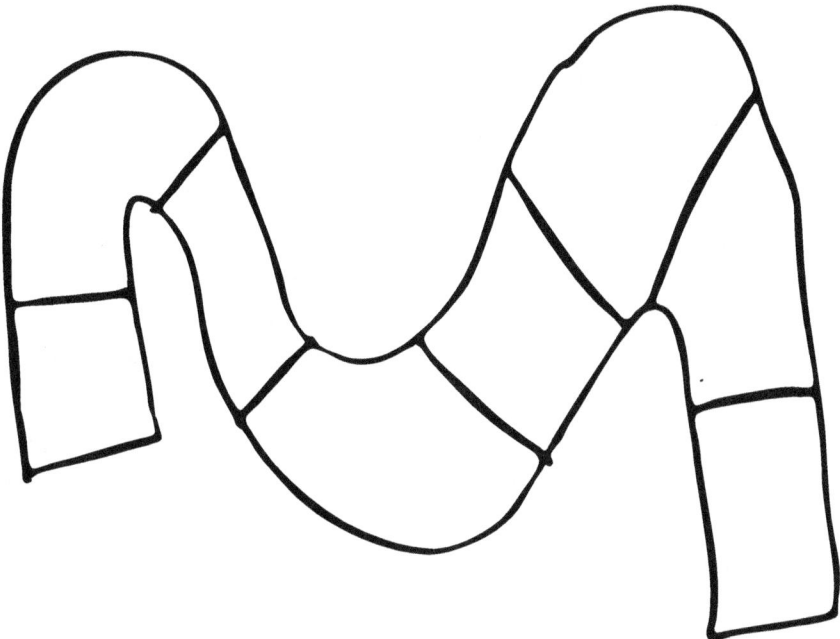

expression of their own stories both visually and verbally. The pathway activity had the unexpected effect of enabling young people to tell more cohesive stories about their aspirations and their plans. In fact, when my colleagues and I presented our research findings at education-centered conferences, we found that it was the pathways images that connected most with audiences.

A BIT OF TABLE-SETTING

The settings for these conversations varied. In some cases, focus groups were held in research facilities. In small towns with no particular facilities, the groups sometimes met in a small hotel or inn. Typically, the research team "over-recruited" to ensure that enough people showed up and met the criteria for participation. Sometimes, twelve to fifteen young people would be gathered in the anteroom (the lobby, waiting room, or similar). My team and I then selected six to eight candidates from this larger group and ushered them into another blank and nondescript room where our focus group conversations, like those you will read below, unfolded.

Groups of this nature are a strange thing. They are organized by people who are often completely external to a community or lived experience. Research participants are often recruited by a third-party agency, as in our case, and based on race, gender, and age. Only later did our research team look at other aspects of participants' backgrounds: the level of education they had completed, the jobs held by their parents, and how they answered an introductory screener question about themselves. Sometimes, participants came from similar socioeconomic backgrounds, and other times, income levels were dramatically different. For example, annual household incomes for some participants were less than $25,000 (i.e., lower-income), others, more than $75,000, and some in between. We made these choices with the intention of creating well-balanced groups in which participants could and would speak from different contexts.

The following conversations with Renee, Maria, Gabriel, and Lyrik took place in Greenville, Mississippi; Belle Glade, Florida; Oakland, California; and New York, New York, respectively. Each group included a mix of young people from the immediate area or from within forty-five minutes of the meeting place by car or public transit. Each participant shared certain characteristics with others in the focus group—namely, race or ethnicity, gender, and approximate age (as described above). After all of the choices we as researchers made to curate the groups and the experience, the groups began in remarkably similar ways. In each location, a small group of strangers were seated at a rectangular table, asked to silence their phones and to share their experiences, ideas, observations, and feelings about their lives, goals, work, and futures.

RENEE

The following pages are excerpts comprised of direct quotes from Renee, a participant in a focus group in Mississippi with young Black women ages eighteen to twenty-one.

I ask that you read Renee's story with care and not become distracted by the elements of her story that may lead you to guess or presuppose what outcomes may lie ahead of her. Listen to the meaning and emotions that Renee brought to her own life experiences. You may be tempted to focus on her pregnancy as the defining inflection point in her young life, but she spoke much more about her relationships with Mississippi, her dreams for herself, and her determination to make good on the invested hopes and dreams of her elders. Renee was motivated and felt supported: she knew where she was going, had a realistic plan to get there, and was looking forward to taking the next step toward her future career.

At the time of the focus group, Renee was eighteen and had recently graduated from high school. She said she received mostly As and Bs in high school, during a period in which she was sent out of state to address some difficulties she was having at school and get back on track. The setting for this focus group was a mostly empty hotel in small-town Mississippi. While none of the young women had ever been in a focus group before, they all settled in quickly and overcame their initial shyness to laugh with and listen attentively to each other.

My name is Renee. I'm eighteen. I stay in Georgia, but I come to Greenville a lot to visit my family.

[I would describe myself as someone who is] . . . respectful, shy, active, helpful, humble, reliable, antisocial, and responsible. Like if anything needs to be done, I'm going to get it done. You can rely on me to get it done.

After like my middle school years, you know, I was getting in trouble every day. Like the . . . test, I didn't pass it at all. I think it was because . . . I was around people I know.

They [other students] used to complain about the clothes I wore, how I had my hair done and my eyes, shoes and stuff. I think it was just because of jealousy. You know, like one day I was getting ready to go home. And . . . by the time I turned the corner, [a] girl hit me in my face. And it was like four or five of them. She got all her friends to jump on me.

If it weren't for my mama, I don't even think I would have graduated. If I would have stayed here.

Like the second semester of school, I moved to Georgia, and like I didn't have no problem. I think me moving helped me out. And I got up there [Georgia], I didn't know anybody.

[In Georgia] I didn't want to talk to nobody, [I was] kind of [a] bully, you know, because you're new to the school. It took me like to my twelfth-grade year to open up to people. . . . we used to have class leaders. . . . they got me to open up to them.

If you a bad person, like don't want to go to school, don't want to do nothing with your life, just sit around, just do nothing, and somebody just comes to you and talks to you about going to school . . . like how you can do this or how you can do that and become a better person. And you listen to that person, and you start going to school, and be something you want to be in life, and you look back to that person, like I'm glad I listened to you. Like if someone talking to you about positive things, that person can just change your whole life around, and you can be a whole new person.

My aunt didn't want to go to school. My grandma sent her to an all-girls' home. That didn't work. And so, like, my granddaddy had stepped up and had talked to her. It was like if you don't do this, this going to happen to you in life. And she listened. She went to school and turned out to be a truck driver.

For Renee, Georgia represented possibility. Georgia was where she was able to make a new start for herself, away from the people she had known in Greenville. She was able to exert control over her social interactions and education and imagine her future in ways that helped her to believe she could, and would, be able to define her life path. The older women in her life had high expectations for her, and she had every intention of meeting those expectations. She was committed to doing better than the generation that preceded her.

Renee's family demonstrated willingness to offer help—her mother had interceded in high school, moving Renee to another state. Her aunt's experience normalized the importance of accepting help and making the most of second chances. Renee framed high school as an opportunity to turn her young life around and start again.

[A career] is something [you] can be happy in what you doing. Something you want to do. Just enjoying what you do—family, more money, traveling.

Once they [kids] get older and go to school they got homework and stuff, and you want to make sure they be in bed at a certain time so they can be ready for the next school day and all that. You going to want to be around your child. My mom used to tell me that her mama missed out on all her high school stuff, [like the] awards ceremony. I wouldn't want to be like that.

My mom, like she do nursing home work, and she sit with like, you know, the old people. My daddy, he transport goods and stuff. You have to pay bills somehow, some way.

The group shared their own and their mothers' experiences growing up with working mothers (participants' grandmothers). They agreed that a good job was one that would allow them to "keep" their children at home and see them grow up.

The moderator asked each person to complete the pathway worksheet. Each participant wrote their goal at one end of the pathway image and placed themselves somewhere on the path relative to that goal. Renee described herself as just beginning to make progress.

FIGURE 1.2 Renee's Pathway Image

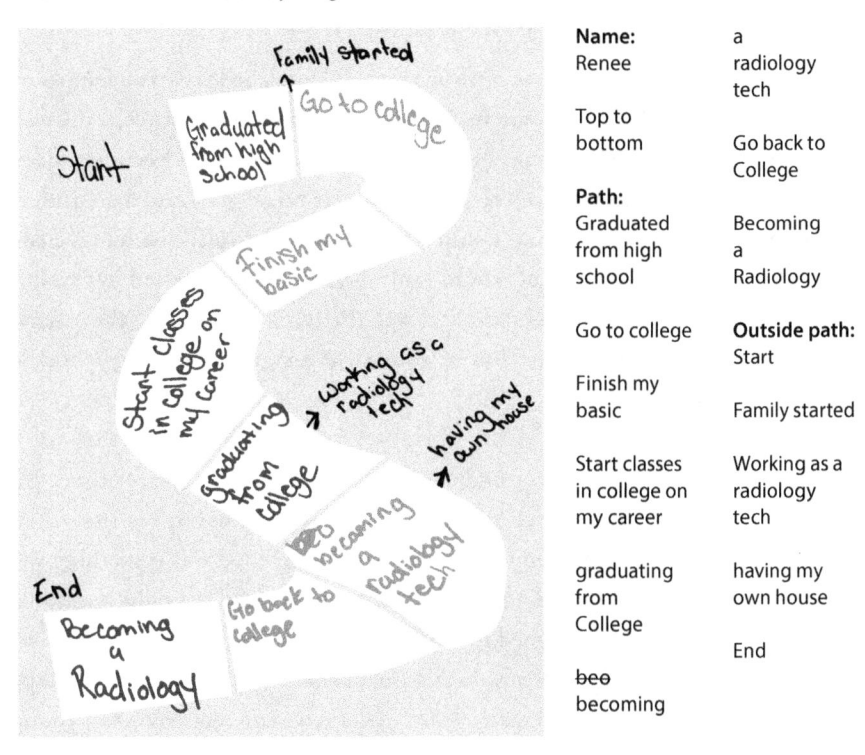

(Handwritten pathway diagram with stepping stones labeled:)
Start → Graduated from high school → Go to college → Family started → Finish my basic → Start classes in college on my career → Graduating from college → Working as a radiology tech → having my own house → becoming a radiology tech → Go back to college → End: Becoming a Radiology

Name: Renee	a radiology tech
Top to bottom	Go back to College
Path:	
Graduated from high school	Becoming a Radiology
Go to college	**Outside path:** Start
Finish my basic	Family started
Start classes in college on my career	Working as a radiology tech
graduating from College	having my own house
~~bee~~ becoming	End

I'm not in school yet. I enroll in January at [two-year college] to be a radiologist technician.

[I'm] graduating. I'm going to go to college to finish up the rest of my basics, because like I took half of my basics in high school. Then start classes for my career. Graduate from college. By the time I'm twenty-five, I plan on being a radiologist tech and staying in Georgia in my own house. I want a house with some stairs. Like when I was younger I used to say I want a maid. But I'd rather do it myself. Yeah, I'd rather have like three cars in my yard with my daughter.

[At] forty-five, I'm moving up in my career. [After I] become a radiologist tech, [I'll] go back to college to be a radiologist, the doctor.

To become a radiologist is nothing but two years, but to become the doctor is like four years. There's a gap in between. I'm not sure how long, but I know I'm going back. I'm going to school in January, so . . . I'm going to get a long start, do what it takes.

Like being a radiologist and being antisocial, you know, it's not going to work. I'm going to have to open up more to people. Talk to people more, come out . . . share. It takes me a while to open up.

> *My mom and grandma, auntie. They can see me like becoming what I want to be in life or being better than them.*

Renee believed her goals were within reach. While she knew the length of time and the specific requirements for becoming a radiologist tech, she was unclear or lacked specificity on how to take the next steps to become a doctor. She knew what she wanted to do, had a near-term goal, and also understood how that near-term goal could lead to other dreams. She had a clear idea of what her environment would look like when she reached her vision of a good life, and she and her daughter were thriving. Renee, like the others, evoked the material construction of a home as a sign of thriving—in this case, a home with stairs.

Renee had made good on her second chance. She was on her way to becoming a mother, a role that she was excited about, in contrast to narratives that often frame pregnancy as a dead end or catastrophe. Motherhood was something she saw as a fact of life, a pothole but not a crater on her path. The fight in middle school and her pregnancy seemed to motivate her—she knew she could do hard things. Her transfer out of state for high school helped her to see she could shape her identity, as well as set and reach goals. Perhaps we can see Renee as a young person already beginning her path with remarkable agency and instincts around self-preservation and personal growth.[3] She was preparing for her adult life as a mother and a professional—fulfilling the hopes and expectations of her mother, auntie, and grandmother.

MARIA

None of the girls in Belle Glade had been part of a focus group before. As the conversation began, they looked expectantly at the moderator, waiting for direction for what would come next. The girls were hesitant, but their hesitancy seemed as if it was also a product of courtesy, a desire to let each person finish her thoughts or sentences before entering the conversation.

As you read, you may find it easy or tempting to see Maria as a young woman who is a typical success story. She had a clear plan for her future and a career goal, and she knew how to get there. Maria's imagined future was deeply connected to her perception of her parents' sacrifice and their expectations for her. Notice how her parents' aspirations influence Maria's own.

In this group, we used an approach where participants sat in pairs for a few minutes, telling one another about themselves. Then, each participant introduced the other to the group. The young woman who introduced Maria said the following, "Maria goes to [four-year college]. She lives with her mom and stepdad, she is majoring in nursing, and she likes to watch Netflix." The remainder of this vignette is drawn from Maria's own words.

> *I am shy, funny, kind. Once I get to know you, I talk a lot, and I am polite. When I was younger I used to get bored a lot in school, so now I try to be as kind as possible to anybody because I know how it feels when you are being talked down to. So, I always have to be kind.*
>
> *Polite—I guess it is how my parents raised me. I have always been taught to respect my elders . . . to be polite. It is just the way I was raised. When I was younger when we would go to the store. I was polite to everybody; the cashier, the person helping. "Oh, your daughter is so polite," and then [my mom] would be like, "oh, thank you.". I won't get rewarded because that is how it is supposed to be. It is just how it is.*

Maria cared about how she was perceived in public and showed deference to her elders and her mother through her behavior. It was important to her that the group understood that it wasn't an act—but central to her identity and how she believed the world worked.

> *I am Mexican American, female. I am Christian, but I just don't like the connotation that comes with it that. [Some people believe] . . . Christians are judgmental. I believe there is a God and I believe everyone is equal. So with the word "Christian" some people would take it that way. Other people take it the other way. And then I am Hispanic. I say Mexican American, I guess. I was born here, that is the only reason why I say Mexican American, because every aspect in my life is Mexican. Like at home we speak Spanish mostly. My grandparents won't speak English even though my mom was born here. So I am second generation Mexican American. She was born here but she was raised in Mexico, so usually . . . we speak Spanish; everything is more Mexican than American.*
>
> *Mexican American . . . more Mexican, actually because I want to raise my kids to speak Spanish, also. My siblings speak Spanish but not as well as I do. Like only a couple words and then my little brother, he doesn't speak any Spanish.*
>
> *I feel like he should. Because I told my mom and stepdad, "Oh, you ought to teach him Spanish." They're like "yeah but he understands it." He doesn't speak it, and I was like "but he needs to speak it." They are the parents; I let them do what they [need to do].*

When Maria and the other seven young women discussed their backgrounds and cultures, they described a wide range of experiences related to their Hispanic identities. Some felt they were white or more white because of how others perceived them. They gave examples such as not tanning, or not speaking Spanish. Those who identified primarily as Americans did so largely based on a lack of Spanish fluency and speaking English at home. They also spoke about the race and culture of their friends; in a notable example, one girl said, "My friends are mostly Cuban, so that makes me feel culturally more Cuban."

> Now more than ever racism is still very real.
>
> I mean I was born here and I had a really bad experience at a mall. And I was born here, so like I can't imagine how . . . immigrants feel when they are talked to that way.
>
> My dad had a really bad experience at work. It was a coworker [who] was American, white. My dad was [working on the plumbing] and the guy told him, "I remember when it used to be the other way around when I was your boss and you guys were working for us." Then my dad didn't say anything, but like he told me about it, and I just felt really bad. Because my dad is an American citizen now, but he started off—he came here illegally. But it is just like it opens my eyes to like we are a small town, and we felt that didn't exist here but apparently it does.
>
> I think it just depends on the person.

Maria had already seen and experienced racism and discrimination. She understood racism as real and also perceived racism to be something that could be overcome because in her experience racism consisted of behaviors perpetrated by individuals. The racism that her father experienced at the mall was an individual experience but was not necessarily systemic. Maria felt that being perceived to be "illegal" was particularly hurtful.

> I think if you work hard enough anybody can achieve whatever they want.
>
> I want to be a registered nurse. I want to have my own place like my own apartment or whatever. I want to be working at a hospital, and I want to travel. I want to take retirement early. A balance between work life and personal life, like a balance. You have enough to support yourself and your family.
>
> Going to college isn't cheap. Like you need a good amount of money, especially for the two-year, four-year degrees.
>
> My dad has always told me. My mom, the same thing—she just wants me to have a job. I want to say she doesn't care if I'm not happy in the job, but I feel she is more

VIGNETTES   25

FIGURE 1.3   Maria's Pathway Image

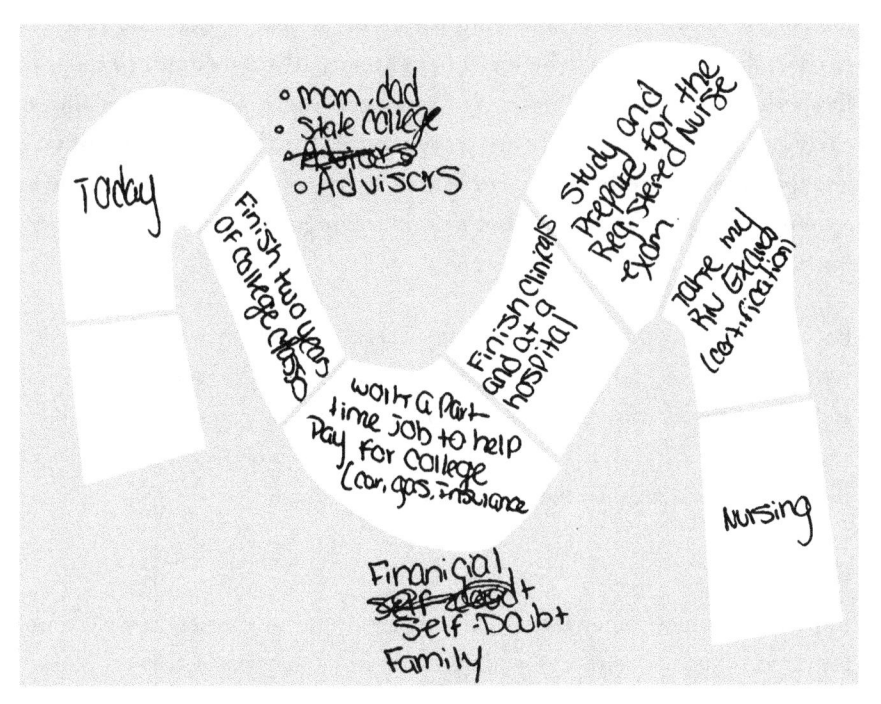

| Name:
Maria
Top to bottom

Path:
Today

Finish two years
of college classes | Work a part
time Job to help
Pay for college
(car, gas, Insurance

Finish Clinicals
and at a
hospital | Study and
Prepare for the
Registered Nurse
exam

Take my
RN Exam
(certification)

Nursing | Outside path:
• Mom - dad
• State College
• ~~Adviors~~
• Advisors

Financial
~~Self - doudt~~
Self-Doubt
Family |

worried about the financial part than me being happy or content in what I'm doing. My dad has always said having a stable job is important but also doing something you love to do is very important also.

My dad tells all my siblings and I, "I work so that you guys can be more than what I am."

That is pressure. I want you to do better than I am. Then you think about what if I fail? Are they going to think I didn't do better, or they are not going to be happy?

Maria felt indebted to her parents, who supported her and her dreams. That support, although positive and helpful, also felt like pressure. She

worried about failure and the tension between doing what you love and making money—and reconciling different messages that she received from each parent. Maria believed her career pathway would, in part, be in service to her parents' journey, work, and sacrifice. Maria's vision of thriving included ownership, travel, work-life balance, and having enough money to retire early. For Maria, thriving was defined not only by an ability to care for oneself but also by caring for those who had cared for her.

For some young people, the stakes for succeeding are higher than others. For young people like Maria, her confidence in the path she had set out for herself, and her strong desire to achieve was deeply influenced by a sense of responsibility and duty to her parents. In this way, her own perception of the good life to which she aspired was shaped by her parents' hopes and dreams.

GABRIEL

In Oakland, it took some time for the group of fifteen- to eighteen-year-old young men to warm up to one another and the moderator. It happens this way at times—for several minutes, the group's actions consisted of one-word answers, muffled laughter between some participants and a feeling that others had completely checked out. From the observation room, I had the impression that some participants were there solely because their parents or a teacher told them to come—that someone had urged them to get the easy money that came with participation. A few beats in—when the moderator asked the group to imagine their future lives at ages twenty-five, forty-five, and seventy-five, Gabriel was the first to begin testing the space. He sprinkled a few curse words into his responses and talked about jobs or careers that could be seen as taboo—growing and distributing marijuana. He, along with the rest of the group wanted to find out if the moderator would interject and try to control the tone of the conversation. The moderator did not intervene.

When this group met, Gabriel was an eleventh grader. Throughout the discussion, he seemed to oscillate between telling the group he had everything figured out about his career and life trajectory and showing the group glimpses of how he was still very much in the process of figuring life out. Gabriel was part bravado and part bluster, but he also described the possibilities of adulthood and career with excitement.[4]

> My name is Gabriel. I live with my mom and my two sisters. I don't work right now. I just like going out, chill with friends.
>
> I am antisocial with new people. I am chunky, like big. I'm funny. I am a jokester. I draw. I can't be at the house. I hate being at the house so I am always out. I like going out all the time. I have a great imagination. I like art too, all around the town. I like graffiti art.
>
> I'm Latino, my whole family. I feel more American than I do Mexican. I am Mexican American, honestly because at the house and anywhere with my family it is always Spanish, Spanish, Spanish. They will be trying to get me into the culture more, the food, the holidays, all of that. I try to get into it more. I try and go out there [to Mexico] too. I am trying to see how it really is. A lot of my family is out there. I wish that I could see them.

When asked about his background and identity Gabriel used mostly positive terms to describe his character and his affect.

> If I get a job, I want it to be temporary. I don't want to be there forever. I want bigger than where I'm at right now. I mean a job is a job. You are just doing it for money, right? I want to work somewhere I want to be happy going. I don't want to wake up mad when I go to work.
>
> When I'm twenty-five and if I've got the money, I am for sure [going to] be growing marijuana. You can grow a little bit for personal use. At twenty-five I will try to own a good car at least, right off the lot. Probably a Mustang if I've got the money by then. Be working at construction; be out clubbing all the time, if I've got money. And racing—I am trying to start racing [cars], too. I am still going to be here by then though. Then at forty-five I own a house, hopefully. Buy a car off the lot like cash; open up my shop; still grow; have kids by then, and I am going to try to learn how to paint cars. I'm trying to see if I can make a boutique/smoke shop. I am trying to travel all over the world and drink like rare bottles.
>
> [A career] It's going to be something that you are going to do for the rest of your life, so you got to love it not hate it. I had a mentor too who was somewhat of a teacher but he didn't like it [teaching] because he would be stressing. It would test his patience. They [students] just disrespect a lot. [When] it's my store, you don't have to worry about nothing. I can do whatever I want.
>
> Even your hobbies that you like doing every day could be your career. And you don't need to go to school for that because I know a lot of people that don't go to college are rich right now.

I look at career [as] being your own boss. That is mandatory. I don't want to work for nobody. I want to work for myself. I want to be my own boss.

It's going to be like a headache getting there because there are going to be a lot of people trying to push you down.

Gabriel drew a clear distinction between a "job" and a "career." He was confident about what constituted a career and the emotional experience he wanted to have as a business owner. He felt that his interests could propel him into a career that he liked and in which he could be successful.

Save up, that is a big thing [and] practice drawing more, just sketch more stuff out. My second step: be more open with people, being more confident about myself; learn the business; learn business in general. You know, like spread out the news to all people what your business is about. Be more like presentable to people. Yeah, a different look—be presentable not just how I came dressed today. I don't want people to think, oh shit I don't want to go to that guy and buy clothing off of him. I feel like, less baggy clothes, cut my hair or something. I don't know, just look presentable, not scary.

Work on whatever is in front of me and not care about other people's opinions. Whatever I've got going on, don't over think it and just do it. Don't care about what one person said and not get distracted. My last step: not getting distracted.

Yeah, and just finding my motivation because just shit that will be going on in people's lives, putting you down. I have just got to ignore that part and just find what makes me happy and makes me want to do it so I can do it.

Gabriel was confident that changes to his person were necessary to succeed in business. He saw himself and a potential lack of motivation as the key barriers to his career goals—in other words, success or failure was mostly, if not entirely, up to him.

Honestly, I can learn from anywhere, but I am trying to go to events, programs at school. There is an event every first of the month where people just gather up and sell clothing or sell whatever. It is like a whole section of people are there. It is a big part [of the culture here]. I met a few people that were cool. They make clothing too. People off the streets I am trying to learn the business off [these people] not people in suits.

People in the streets know what people in the street want; people in suits don't know what people out here like. I look to my people and ask them straight up how it is.

Gabriel was passionate about his art and having realized this could be a career path, was actively seeking out and accumulating more information

about how adult artists made a living in his city. Through attending the city event he was networking and gaining exposure to people who could become his professional peers and his consumers. He had found a way into the professional and creative community he hoped to become a part of one day.

> *[How does it feel when people tell you about your strengths?] It depends who tells me. If it is somebody really close to me, somebody who really knows me, then I will understand. I will just sit back and just think, oh that's true. But if it is somebody I just met, I'm like, "Hell no!" I don't like that.*
>
> *[There are] three teachers out of my whole school that I really like. They just get me. They get how I work. Instead of talking about what you are doing, they are on your side. They hear you out. They try to help you. I take it cool what [those] teacher[s] tell me.*
>
> *[What about your weaknesses, like you being impatient or lazy] When you get tired of people saying it so much, you've got to step back and just think on it. Don't be—have a hard head about it.*

Gabriel was self-aware and knew that he had issues and weaknesses. He recognized that there were parts of himself he would need to confront as he pursued his path, and he had a small group of adults with whom he could confide.

LYRIK

As you read Lyrik's story, you may notice a lot of negativity and pessimism in his words, which may sound like resignation. While I understand where that interpretation comes from, I heard Lyrik describe a clear sense of and desire to have agency in his own life. He was oriented toward *thriving* despite his negativity.

At the time of the focus group, Lyrik was eighteen years old and a senior in a New York City high school. He was younger than some of the other young men in the room but still a powerful contributor to the focus group.

> *My name is Lyrik. I work [stocking shelves]. I live with my mom and my ten-year-old brother.*
>
> *I feel like my mom expects me to go out and run the world. She's the most positive one. She says that I can do whatever I want to do. She says her job is to get me to the point where I can do whatever [I] want and I feel like that's supportive. I know that my mom has my back in public. She will never let anything happen that will set me back.*

FIGURE 1.4 Lyrik's Pathway Image

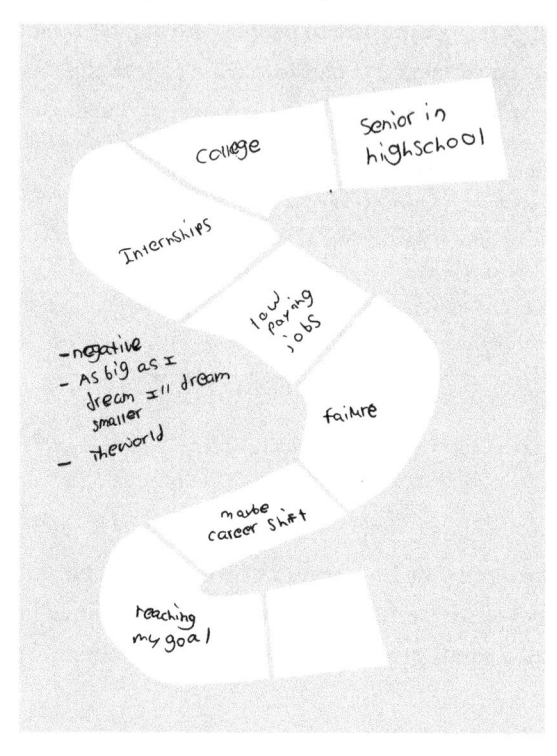

Name: Lyrik	failure
Top to bottom	maybe career Shift
Path: Senior in high school	reaching my goal
college	**Outside path:** −negative
Internships	−As big as I dream Ill dream smaller
low paying jobs	−The world

During the two-hour focus group, Lyrik never mentioned his father. In contrast, his single mother was omnipresent, his advocate, and also a reminder of the professional and life struggles that Lyrik hoped to avoid.

> *Career is the endgame, lifestyle, money, life, college, and in it for the long run. Like it shouldn't be like the first thing you do. It's the last stop on the train. It's not a job. It's not work. It's what you're going to do for the rest of your life.*
>
> *For me, the adults in my life are like people I have to surpass. Because like I love my mom. She supports me, you know, everything, but she's not doing what she set out to do. Like she got her degree. She has a master's. But she don't do that, and neither do her brothers and sisters. They didn't go to college. And life just beat them down, I think. One is a drug addict. So it's like for me, I have to do it to surpass them and be better than them. Like I don't want to follow in their footsteps. I want to be ten times better than them.*
>
> *I've seen my mom struggle. I know what struggle is. Like when my mom goes to the grocery store, she's like how much does this cost? How much does [that]cost? I know that sounds petty, but I don't want to do that. I want to be able to live and do whatever I want to do.*

Lyrik was talking about the quality of life he saw his mother living, not her specific profession or career. He noticed that his mother did not have "enough," in this case, money, and he saw the connection between having enough money and having choices. Lyrik rejected some of the qualities of surviving at a job that he had experienced up until that point, and was figuring out how he might determine what steps he would need to take to reach his own version of a "good life."

My [pathway] is a little generic because I'm not really sure yet. But for right now, starting off as a senior in high school, college, maybe after college if I decide to go, internships because, you know, you got to build up yourself while you're doing that. A low-paying job, you know, because you got to start off somewhere at the bottom usually. You don't just jump to the top immediately. I expect myself to make a mistake somewhere along the line and maybe a career shift. Like maybe change my mind somewhere down the middle, maybe not. And then eventually, reaching my goal at the end.

[Do you know what your goal is?] No.

There are programs that you can take that can help you achieve your goals. Theater program classes and creative writing classes that you can take while in high school. There are also certified courses in some of the colleges where you can get certifications without getting a degree.

For me, twenty-five would look like probably living in a crappy apartment somewhere in the five boroughs. I'll have roommates. One of them is probably going to be a little smelly. I'm living in the five boroughs. I'm going to need some roommates. Rent is expensive . . . what am I going to be doing? I don't know. Probably be going to school or just got out of like whatever, who knows, maybe, maybe not, maybe still working, maybe didn't go, don't know. Maybe I'm still working, and maybe I didn't go to college or whatever. And I'll probably be just like supporting my family.

[At age seventy] probably living in Long Island . . . like deep, deep away from the five boroughs. One of those . . . nice little fairytale towns. I got grandkids. I've got my own thing going on. It may not be my own business, but I've got my own thing. Probably maybe if I'm doing something for someone else, probably like I have oversight, but I still do my own thing most of the time and check in every now and then. Seventy, I'm probably not working, probably retired at that point. But I may still have like a limited role in whatever I'm doing. I want to be able to live and do whatever I want to do. And you got to be an entrepreneur to do that. You got to have your own. You can't be making money for other people to do that.

The barriers would be like my own negativity. It's like as big I dream, I'll dream even smaller. Like I can have that mansion, but at the same time, I'm going to be living in that crack house by forty.

I have to work on positivity. For me, being negative is like the easiest thing for me to do. Like I can sit here and tell you like seven negative things just from sitting here.

In the previous excerpt Lyrik was thinking about the quality of the life that he hoped to one day lead—he was sure of how it would feel to thrive, but he was not sure how to get there. Lyrik was self-aware, and shared that he knew he would have to conquer his negativity to survive. He was also outwardly aware that resources, beyond college, existed that could help him to transition from high school and into adulthood. And yet, he didn't understand how to relate these resources to his own life.

I'm the only Black kid at school and I've had a very hard life. Me, I've seen my mom struggle. I know what struggle is, and I handle it. So I feel like Black people have to struggle, like struggle. When crap hits the fan, it hits hard. So I feel like we understand that better than other races, something like that.

[In response to another participant saying the "the white man" is the biggest barrier that he will face as he works to reach his own goals.] Everybody's coming for us. The Asian man, the Indian man, the dude at the corner, everyone coming for you. For me, like I go to a mostly Asian school, and when their daughters are getting picked up, they can't be seen with me because their parents would be like, who is that negro next to you? And same with the Indian ones, everyone. It's tough because they can't be seen with you. They're best friends in school, but as soon as they walk out, who are you? It's crazy.

[What's important to you at twenty-five?] Twenty-five? Making it to twenty-six.

Lyrik was aware of and had already experienced racism in multiple dimensions and at multiple times. These experiences, at school and elsewhere, informed his perception of how race functions in the world, and also his expectations for how his Blackness could influence his future pathway.[5]

SURVIVING, STRIVING, AND THRIVING

You may have found some common themes and patterns throughout these stories in what you have read so far. You have likely noticed that Renee, Maria, Gabriel, and Lyrik were already making choices that would impact their future lives and drive their path and career trajectories. Perhaps you posited that these choices were deeply influenced by their identities, cultures, beliefs, and environments. Whether they were high school students, out of school and working, or attending college or another type of post-secondary education at the time these focus groups took place, many focus group participants saw the choices and steps they had already taken as evidence of both their own agency and a feeling that the journey toward their futures had already begun.[6]

As we listened to young people, like the four you have gotten to know in this chapter, my colleagues and I began to see patterns in how they thought about and experienced education and work. We could see the emotional connections they associated with different phases of their educations, and how they thought about desirable life outcomes and the choices that would get them there. With the help of a cognitive linguist who works to identify metaphors that anchor and influence how people speak and communicate, we were able to codify these patterns in a framework–*Surviving, Striving, and Thriving*.[7] Most importantly, the framework sought to describe both the feelings young people assigned to the experiences they'd had so far and how they characterized these different work states; in other words, what they expected to experience in each state. Perhaps most crucially, the framework enabled us, as researchers, to describe work and career as a continuum, reflecting young people's assertion that work was a fixed destination, a goal, and also a journey through overlapping and interconnected emotional states.

At one end of the continuum is *surviving*. *Surviving* means having to struggle and work hard just to meet basic needs. When *surviving*, young people are working jobs they feel they have to do to make ends meet, and they are living paycheck to paycheck. *Surviving* is characterized by having little to no control over when, how much, or how little you work.

The middle state is *striving*. It functions as a precursor to *thriving*. *Striving* is a state of mind where young people feel that they have goals and they are intentionally following a set of steps that they believe will help them to achieve their goals. When striving, young people are making decisions and acquiring the knowledge, skills, experiences, and connections that they will need to refine or reach the goals they have set for themselves. For those who could articulate the components of *striving*, it was understood to be a combination of personal effort and specific steps toward a career goal. When young people engage with the ideas around *striving*, they describe perseverance, struggle, having patience with oneself, and seeking out and completing more education.

At the other end of the continuum is the experience of *thriving*. When young people experience a state of *thriving*, they feel they have achieved their personal goals. When they are *thriving*, young people see themselves in careers they love or find fulfilling, allowing them to live their personal version of a good life.

Each of the young people you've met in this chapter were oriented toward *thriving*. They aspired to be stable, have some control over their time and labor, contribute to or pay back their community or family, own a house or a business—to have "enough." Enough money to live or to travel, enough work to be independent, enough money, time, space to not be just getting by. Sometimes, their dreams were incredibly specific: Renee, planning for her future with her child and her future career in radiology, imagined a life in which she owned her own house, had a yard, and three cars for herself and her daughter. She described the house as having stairs, contrasting with the double-wide trailers that peppered the countryside of small towns and rural areas in Mississippi and Georgia.

Gabriel also dreamed of having control. Working for himself, having his own business, and being his own boss. He wanted to have enough money, feel the freedom and fun of his twenties, and achieve some measure of independence. But he also saw his twenties as a phase, one that would end as he transitioned to more adult responsibilities of starting and being successful in business. Gabriel saw himself first as an artist—an identity and career path. He imagined the expression of his art would evolve over time, from the sketching he was doing as a high school student to the car art he anticipated doing in his twenties to the small clothing and marijuana boutique he hoped to run in the future.

Maria and Lyrik also aimed to thrive, committed to making their parents proud or surpassing them somehow—another facet of thriving. Maria wanted to be a daughter worthy of the investment made by her parents and on her behalf. Her thriving was characterized by having enough money to be able to support her family and herself and to be able to travel. And Lyrik's thriving was not worrying about the cost of groceries, not struggling as he has seen his mother do, but instead to "live and do whatever I want to do."

"IT'S ALL UP TO ME"

In the context of striving, the young people in these focus groups and elsewhere in the research project felt like the success or failure of their future lives was "all up to me." They felt alone in making decisions about their educational and career pathways, with little or no support from adults or others. Many knew they would need support to reach their goals, but few knew where to find it.

As they reached toward the future career and life goals that would enable them to experience a sense of thriving, they were sometimes burdened by the responsibility they had assigned themselves. When Gabriel talked about the things that could stand in the way of his success, he focused almost entirely on himself—caught up in other people's perceptions of him, and lacking motivation.

With Maria, we heard the pressure of trying to fulfill parental dreams and the worry about inexplicably failing. When Lyrik said his mom wanted more for him than what she had and that she has always struggled, he was also expressing the difficulty of trying to avoid not only a life of struggle but also the near-crushing burden of not knowing how to avoid it.

Parents, particularly mothers, were often a source of support and motivation in young people's lives. However, other adults, particularly those who could provide guidance as they pursued their education and careers, were mentioned less frequently. The teachers at Gabriel's school that he felt "got" him and the familial elders who had helped Renee leave a harmful middle school environment and move to Georgia were the exceptions and not the rule.

Young people in this chapter and the research more broadly overwhelmingly wanted to and believed they could thrive in work and career. Differences lay in how equipped they felt to set specific goals for themselves, how they conceptualized and thought about the steps that would lead them to their goals, and how confident they were that they had or could locate the information, resources, and people they would need to make progress toward their goals.

In some cases, young people characterized their steps toward their imagined futures as relational or having to do with building relationships with others. This looked and sounded like networking, internships, and otherwise needing people to get their foot in the door. Others framed their steps as emotional—focused on self-growth, a desire to become different from who they are now, to be more mature, more courageous, or more confident. Finally, some saw the steps as instructional—having to do with getting degrees, certificates, accreditation, or completing some form of academic coursework. Most pathway images were dominated by one or two types of steps—for example, a pathway had more relationships and instructional steps than emotional ones. How young people described these stepping stones gives us a glimpse into their perception of how the world works and their place in it.

For Gabriel, the steps were emotional and relational. For him, the path consisted of improvements he believed he needed to make to his physical appearance and the relationships he needed to build. He wanted to be taken seriously by other artists. Gabriel's steps also revealed something else: he believed he needed to accumulate different types of experiences in the different contexts that touched his dream career and life. He felt he needed to experience how it felt to work as an artist, to build a business, and to be an entrepreneur. It is the collection of these experiences that he believed would result in the skills he needed to succeed in his chosen career. And, for him, these experiences held far greater currency than college.

For Renee and Maria, the steps toward their future lives were informational—a series of certificates and degrees that would help them move from where they were now to the job or career they wanted first. And then there was Lyrik. If we look closely, Lyrik, too, was building an early on-ramp to his path. He assumed that there would be some amount of trial and error necessary before he figured out what step to take next. In his pathway image he included steps like finding an internship, building himself up; getting a low-paying job, and making a mistake and learning from it. Lyrik was actively refining his steps in real time, collaborating with the other young men in the group to determine what step might come next.

WORK AS A MEANS TO AN END

Renee, Maria, Gabriel, and Lyrik wanted to live a *good life*, and they saw a good job as a means to having the life they envisioned for themselves. They understood that their journeys toward the *good life* they desired would be characterized by a mix of personal and work experiences, and most expected that they would have to strive for some amount of time before thriving. Work for these young people was a means to get to thriving—not thriving itself. Importantly it was the minority of young people who spoke about the end of their pathway in terms of what they would be doing for work or the name or title of the job. Instead, the end of the pathway was described in terms of how it would feel to experience whatever their version of success looked like.

I imagine this is the case for many of us reading this book. A career for many is often not a deeply held passion. Instead (and certainly no less important or valuable), work affords us something we want for our lives—the opportunity to experience *thriving*. The ability to take care of family, the freedom to do the things that excite us or interest us, the ability to pay for the home we own or rent, to put food on the table—to have enough.

Think back to these stories. Radiology, for Renee, was a career that would enable her to provide herself and her daughter with the stability they needed and the time and control of her schedule that would allow her to see her child grow up. Maria wanted to provide for her family. They all wanted a *good life*, and a *good job* was key to achieving that life.

I chose to share these individual stories because, as helpers, we tend to lean into the aggregate—whether by training or default, we crave the scalability of numbers. I wanted to cut through the noise and focus on four individual young people and four short stories before transitioning into the overwhelm and dynamism of the more complicated focus group. I wanted you to hear them as they considered and spoke about the different paths that lay ahead.

In the next two chapters, you'll get to know the other young men who participated in Lyrik's focus group in New York. We'll hear from them how they experience work and life at different points on the *Surviving, Striving, and Thriving* continuum and explore how they define a *good life* and the steps they believe will lead them there.

CHAPTER 2

Listening to One Group in New York

In the previous chapter, I invited you to listen to four young people's opinions, experiences, and aspirations. These stories from the more than forty focus groups we conducted represent only an inkling of the richness of the full dataset. My goal in this approach is to enable you to meet and engage with individual voices and catch a glimpse of these young people on their own terms. But responding to the invitation to listen may not be that easy. Simply presenting a single-voice vignette only provides a snapshot of context, and while that's fine for some readers, for others, it might have felt like I asked you to climb a wall in the dark. Whenever we are asked to engage differently, we don't always know how to approach or make meaning of what we are experiencing. In this chapter, I pull away from the vignettes and lean into the focus group themselves, providing the interactive, conversational context in which stories emerged and I will also share my own observations about the group and the young participants. The previous chapter was an invitation to engage with individual stories; this chapter and the one that follows help move between the story created by a single individual and the narratives created by the group.

We will delve more deeply into the metaphor of 'work as a journey' and the conceptual framework of *Surviving, Striving, and Thriving*, and how concepts around work and career emerge within a single focus group. In particular, we'll explore how the notions of *Surviving* and *Thriving* connect to young people's personal and observed work experiences and how this first-hand knowledge influences their emerging occupational identities—how they see themselves, what they feel they are good at doing, and where they feel they belong: it sets a process in motion that includes accepting, modifying, or rejecting those experiences to better understand what opportunities to seek out. As you listen to the young people you meet in this chapter, I encourage you to be patient—they are just starting to explore their own possibilities. Listen for the myriad ways in which young people see themselves as the most important agent of change in their own lives, the connections they make between their identities and their future lives, and the relationships they build to inspire and support them as they make their way into the unchartered waters of adulthood. Finally, I encourage you to read passages more than once—turn their words over in your mind, give yourself permission to drop into the cadence of their voices, the overlapping ideas, the riffs that describe the goals they've set for themselves, and the stepping stones they believe will help them forge their paths.

As I've written earlier in this book, narratives are a form of power. Narratives, the themes embedded within the stories we tell, inform and shape the way we make meaning of the world around us, and help us to understand why things are the way they are and whether and how we as individuals can change them. In the United States, there is often a striking disconnect between the prevailing narratives about young Black men and the personal realities they live and experience. Black men experience a paradox in the American racial imagination—overlooked and dismissed in some respects while hypervisible and subjected to constant surveillance in others.[1] In philanthropy, research, and education policy contexts, narratives about young Black men are ever-present. It is often one of stress, oppression, and trauma, most often underpinned by stories that highlight disparities in health, education, and income, among others.[2] First-person stories about young Black who are unremarkable by societal standards, for instance, men who are not preternaturally gifted in sports, entrepreneurial skill, or academics, are almost entirely absent.

It is this absence of stories—the primary element of narratives—that led me to anchor this chapter around and within a group of young Black men in New York City. The group included participants between the ages of seventeen and twenty-one who were not currently enrolled in post-secondary education and had decided, for the moment, not to attend college. Because they belonged to a group that receives a great deal of focus from those who develop policy and programmatic solutions to improve career preparation and support, it felt particularly important to create space in these pages to see and hear from them directly, so we may insert these young people's intelligence and their sense of possibility into the consciousness of those who aim to help them.[3]

SETTING THE SCENE AND INTRODUCTIONS

In chapter 1, you met Lyrik, a young man approaching high school graduation, on the cusp of adulthood, who struggled with confidence and felt unsure of what was to come next. Lyrik was one of eight young men who sat together, talking about their first jobs, the realities of entering adulthood, and how it felt to imagine their future lives, how they saw themselves, what skills they believed they had, and where they felt they belonged.

Before diving into sections of the conversation, it may be helpful to know more about how focus groups like this one are formed and get a sense of the places in which they are conducted.

Public opinion researchers often ride the coattails of the multibillion-dollar, for-profit research and marketing industry and infrastructure. The for-profit sector has developed a robust system for reaching and recruiting diverse people from all over the country, and my colleagues and I often use its research panels to locate research participants who may otherwise not be available to us. Focus group facilities are intentionally nondescript. They are often tucked away in strip malls, mildly deserted shopping centers, or drab office buildings. Their names usually incorporate words such as "perspective," "point-of-view," or "facts," but rarely the word "research." This often obscures the purpose of the building from the public, providing some measure of privacy to participants entering the facility. If participants are under eighteen, they are accompanied by a parent or guardian who consents for their child to participate in the group and then waits in the lobby during the session. If applicable, the participant and their parent receive a monetary token of appreciation for their participation.

The building is designed in such a way as to make you feel that yours is the only group in the facility at any given time. Sometimes, even the bathroom you use is reserved for your group. This is intentional. The facility is set up to feel neutral, even antiseptic. The participants are strangers to one another, and the separation helps to maintain confidentiality.

Lyrik's group took place at a focus group facility in New York City. The young people and the moderator identified as Black. The participants were male; I, the moderator, am female. Water, soda, and snacks were arranged on a table in the corner of the room. Each place was set with a napkin, pen, and pad of paper.

On an evening in November, 2018, eight young men, including Lyrik, walked into the room holding name tents. They chose their own seats at the table, and once seated, I introduced myself and some norms around confidentiality and anonymity. Their conversation began—where all conversations begin—with introductions. What's your first name? Are you studying or working or doing something else? Who lives with you at your home? I have added contextual details where they aid meaning and removed or replaced identifying information.

CEDRIC: *Hi, my name is Cedric. I work at Burger King. And I live with my mom and my dad and my brother.* [At the time, Cedric was in high school.]

LAMAR: *My name is Lamar. I'm twenty years old. I'm an actor. And I live with my mother.*

MALCOLM: *[I'm] Malcolm. Twenty-one. I work in fashion. And I live with roommates pretty much. [I'm] a stylist so for photo shoots or personal shoppers or stuff like that.*

LYRIK: *My name is Lyrik. I work stocking shelves. And what else did you want to know? I live with my mom.* [Lyrik was a senior in high school.]

ALI: *Hello, my name is Ali. I'm eighteen right now, and I coach football at the Boys and Girls Club as like a job. And I live with my mom and my brother right now.*

LUKAS: *My name is Lukas. I'm twenty-one years old. I do construction work. It's like a family business type of thing. And . . . I live with my cousins.*

XAVIER: *My name is Xavier. I'm nineteen, and I work as a sales associate at GameStop. And I live with family.*

MILES: *My name is Miles. I'm nineteen years of age. And I'm a sales associate as well. And I freelance as a model. I live with my mom and my sisters.*

RETURNING TO SURVIVING, STRIVING, AND THRIVING

In the previous chapter, I introduced you to the *Surviving, Striving, and Thriving* framework. *Surviving, Striving, and Thriving* is a thematic and analytical framework that shows the emotional and aspirational states young people pass through and expect to pass through as they pursue the career and life goals they set for themselves. These states are not fixed points; rather, they flow into each other as young people learn, personally or indirectly, about occupational options, make occupational choices, and experience progress and setbacks in their occupational journeys.

The framework is also a continuum in which young people experience greater agency and self-efficacy in their own lives as they move away from *striving* and toward some measure of *thriving*. Underpinning the framework are the words that young people use to describe work and working; from *jobs* worked in the present to survive to the earliest glimpses of the *careers* they believe will provide them with the resources to live the life to which each aspires.

By design, a thematic framework helps us see patterns, relationships, concepts, and interactions across a dataset. Sometimes, it is imposed on the data, and sometimes, as here, it emerges from the data. Across the focus groups, *surviving* is characterized by an inability to control one's time, energy, or talents. In contrast, *thriving* is characterized by having choices and time, owning one's home or business, and the experience of having "enough."

Over the next two chapters, you will accompany this group, as I did, as they first describe what it feels like at both ends of the continuum—*surviving* and *thriving*, and later in chapter 3, map out and discuss the "how" of moving out of a state of *surviving* and into a state of *striving*. We will hear from them directly, in their words, about the steps, stages, opportunities, and people that they believe they will need to move from where they were on a November day to where they want to go.

During the conversation, two specific moments jumpstarted our thinking about a continuum of the personal and emotional experiences of work: an early group discussion about their understanding of the words associated with occupation—job, work, and career, and their meanings, and later, an imagination exercise in which each participant painted a picture for the group of their future lives at ages twenty-five and forty-five.

We'll start with the first moment—the participants' exploration of occupational language.

The group has just been asked to complete a top-of-mind exercise in which they write words, images, ideas, and phrases they associate with the words job, work, and career on a sheet of paper. In this group most participants had received a high school degree or, like Xavier, had received a GED. Only Lyrik and Cedric were still in high school. Everyone in the group was currently working.

In this group, everyone feels they are working to make ends meet or to help out at home. Some are doing "day jobs"—jobs taken out of necessity—while still exploring how to get to the "real work" of living. Entry-level jobs in retail or food service had given them their first taste of working. These first jobs, done as teenagers and very young men, were full of meaningless tasks, annoying people, discomfort, pressure, and stress. While they fulfilled an immediate need, everyone wanted something better for themselves.

CEDRIC: *Job means like . . . Burger King. It is stressful. Working at Burger King is horrible. I hate Burger King. The customers is rude. You miss one thing, they [are] going crazy.*
XAVIER: *Can you make sure my fries are warm?*
MILES: *They are a pain in the ass.*
LAMAR: *When I look at a job that's like 'I got to get a job to pay the bills.' I'm with them. It's stressful. It's, you know, 9:00 to 5:00. You got to do it to pay the bills.*
LUKAS: *Like, okay, like a job is basically something that you feel like you have to do. Like you're pressured or stressed to do. I just feel like jobs are just like a distraction to what your real work is supposed to do while you're living.*

Their feelings about work were also informed by watching older adults around them. Some young men had grown up with parents and other adults working at jobs, or sometimes even careers, that felt unfulfilling or unimportant. These older adults' emotions about their own work lives acutely influenced the boys and young men to chart their own occupational courses in rejection of the choices made by parents and family members, and in service of building a different working reality for themselves.

LUKAS: *Like the people in my life that like adult-wise . . . there's probably like one person in my family that's like I guess you could say living good or like happy with their job. But everybody else is just . . .*
XAVIER: *Depressed.*
LUKAS: *Not even depressed, they're just not happy. . . . I see it in them . . . it's just changes my whole perspective about life, and what I want for myself. Everybody is really just working to get by. They're working in a job that they don't like. They're just working just to work, but nobody is really like following their passions. Nobody is doing what they're supposed to do. Nobody sees, I don't know. People see*

life as . . . work. And it's just not. Like it's clearly not. I just feel like I'm around nothing.

LUKAS: *Like a lot of people in my family they have their degrees. They went to school. They have master's, you know, or bachelor's or whatever. But they're not working in their field. So I know they're not happy. They tell me they're not happy. I see it on their face. Like they always complain about money, complain about this like there's just no fulfillment, no satisfaction in their life as far as work. So it's like I don't know. It's just they're like stagnant.*

ALI: *Because I feel like a lot of people go to college, and they push college a lot, but like a lot of people don't even work in what they studied for.*

LUKAS: *It's insane.*

ALI: *They're like my mom. She did like political science or something, but she don't do that.*

When Lukas describes the jobs and work lives he's seen around him as stagnant, several others chime in, relaying stories—like Ali's—of parents and older family members who tried to change the course of their lives by getting a new or different job, or going to college, but were unable to, and continued to just get by despite their efforts to do something more. Lukas and others saw these adults as trapped by their jobs and their choices. These lived experiences of watching adults with partial and completed college degrees not working out as promised, increased their perception that the only way out of a bad job was to rely on oneself and one's own acumen. In a few cases, parents or other adults explicitly told participants not to follow in their footsteps and to avoid their same struggles or difficulties. This type of guidance and honesty was motivating in its own way.

CEDRIC: *My dad pushed me to be better than him because my dad dropped out of school at a young age. He was like don't be like me, finish, do what you like to do. Because he was at a standstill for about a good 20 years not making no more money. He was at a standstill job.*

ALI: *Yeah, that sounds like me. My dad dropped out of school too. He was kind of young. And he's always telling like I want you to be better than me . . . because he says like working for like, the white man, is like, you get nothing. Like he doesn't want me to do that. So he's telling me like right now to like start figuring out what I want to do and work for that now because you don't want to be working for other people because you're not going to get nothing.*

Some of the young men in this group had also received positive exposure to working life through parents, aunts and uncles, and older cousins. When describing and reflecting on these early exposures to what it felt like to work, these participants would "accept" (i.e., they wanted to do something similar to the work of the adults around them) or "modify" (i.e., they liked or appreciated some aspect of the work that the adults around them did and wanted to incorporate this into their own work lives) the work experiences they'd witnessed as opposed to "rejecting" the work experiences, as discussed above. When participants were asked if they knew anyone with jobs they found appealing, the following unfolded:

CEDRIC: *Yeah, my aunt travels for her job. I don't know [what she does], but she be traveling all over. She is always somewhere else. Like she was in Chicago, Los Angeles, all of that.*

MALCOLM: *Mine is my cousin. He owns two salons. He's killing it right now. He's a hairdresser. And just to see that as a black man just owning your own two businesses, running strong, it's a very motivating thing. Right now, I'm not a hairdresser, but it just helps me, makes me want to be in that same kind of, it just makes me want to push harder.*

When the group began to talk about "work," in earnest, the conversation changed. I got powerful impressions, from every member of the group, of the agency and the excitement they felt about their possible future lives. They talked about work in terms of the value it enabled them to bring to their communities and to themselves. And in this transition, a hierarchy of opinion began to emerge: a job sits at the bottom rung—performed out of necessity, to survive, which many of them felt they were just barely doing. They saw *jobs* as something one has to do. *Work*, on the other hand, was something different. *Work* implied movement—that you were headed somewhere you wanted to go, that you were doing something meaningful. *Work* was understood as both a verb and a noun. When they talked about *work*, their language reflected a sense of *striving*, rather than *surviving*—and I heard their goals, interests, and sense of agency over their life's direction emerge much more clearly than before. Whereas the jobs they held at that time seemed to have little or nothing to do with their dreams, *work* is where they saw their identities, their beliefs, and aspirations begin to shine through.

When Lamar and Malcolm describe *work*, they move away from the transactional language associated with *job* (i.e., something is being done with your labor), and toward language that suggests some measure of self-efficacy.

LAMAR: *For work I put freedom. Basically, when I look at a job it's like I got to get a job to pay the bills. But when I think of work, like with acting, this is for my, you know, my self-interest, my self-gain. You know, self-discipline, passion, goals. So I have that type of mindset for work. But a job can also be an on-ramp if you're lucky. A job can help you to learn something about yourself, to meet the people who can provide the next opportunity.*

MALCOLM: *I agree with everything that they're saying. But I also feel like a lot of people that have a job, end up finding the work. Meaning like without the job, you wouldn't be able to find the work because there's sometimes where people will come into your job that you would never expect to come into your job, and this can change your whole entire life. So I feel like jobs are a necessity, but I feel like depending on how long you keep that job, now, you can always take that job and turn it into work. For some people who are like working in retail who do a sales associate, but if they like the job, they turn into their career. And so now they're management and so forth and so on. So I just feel like a job is definitely a necessity. Granted, all that stuff comes with it.*

But I feel like, without a job, you couldn't get the work. I'm not saying that you can't get the work straight [away] if you're privileged like that. But guess what, most Black folks ain't privileged like that. So in that case, we have to get the job to get to the work.

As the group's conversation about work became more aspirational, the delineation between the *jobs* they had at that time—for survival—and the *work* they felt motivated to do to satisfy their own curiosity and goals became more apparent. Malcolm and Lamar begin to make a departure from working at a job as a cog in a wheel and began to describe a job as an enabler, an entry point or an opportunity.[4] Others were busy making connections between their day-to-day work and the career they wanted to have in the future. Even carving out time to think about and, in some cases, participate in the communities of workers among their chosen professions or careers. This was especially clear with group members already pursuing creative careers like Malcolm, the stylist, and Lamar, the actor. Because they were already earning income through something akin to the work they wanted to do longer term, their jobs were relegated to a side hustle and were therefore less central to their lives. During the introduction, Lamar introduced himself as an actor despite having a day job similar to others in the group. He acknowledged the day job merely by saying "clocking out" to denote the time spent at a job that was of little consequence to his future life. That *job* was not his *work*.

LAMAR: *Whatever time I have between when I clock out and until the sun go down. That's all valuable time. And for some [of] us our work hours is different. But I know for me, like as soon as I clock out, I'm on the phone with this person. All right, where's this audition at? Who can I talk to about this? It's all, it's a network game.*

The more hours you spend wasting it at your job, you'd be like, damn. I could have did this. I could have did that. So it definitely is like kind of what you were saying, modern-day slavery. You know, if you look at it like that, it is. You know, you wake up to pay the bills and go to work to pay the bills. But the moment we clock out, that's when it becomes, all right, it's work. We're working on our own goals. We're working on our own, you know, personal goals.

At the other end of the continuum of occupational language is the word *career*. Careers are broadly perceived as the opposite of the jobs people clock in and out of and are characterized by having the control they lack in their current jobs. Malcolm and other participants share the words and phrases they associate with 'career' below.

MALCOLM: *I put life, family, love, passion, pain in the ass, and full. I feel like . . . by the time you get to your career, your life should be full. Like you've eaten so much [in your] job and then work. [It's like] eating buffets . . . and by the time it gets to the career, you're just full. So it's just a [sense of] fulfillment. I'm here. I made it. It's done. I'm just full.*

LYRIK: *For me, I put endgame, lifestyle, money, life, college, and in it for the long run. It shouldn't be the first thing you do. It's the last stop on the train. You get it? Like it's nowhere else. It's not a job. It's not work. It's what you're going to do for the rest of your life.*

ALI: *Endgame of life.*

MALCOLM: *But, see a career is not really a job.*

CEDRIC: *Yeah, it's not. It's what you would like to do.*

MALCOLM: . . . *if you were in a career that you hate doing, that means there's something wrong somewhere.*

XAVIER: . . . *if you're angry at your career, it's not what you wanted. You need to find something else you want to do . . . [a career is] what you get to do, your passion, give and take, no anger or animosity towards your job or towards the people you work with. This is what you wanted and what you made of it. So you shouldn't be angry at what you decided to make of it.*

The group understood a career to be something fulfilling. They don't have to love doing it, but it has to have some meaning. When Xavier says, "you shouldn't be angry at what you decided to make of it" he leans into the feeling that a career is a choice. Compare that to all the ways this group felt a job was something that happened to you—it was something that you had to do, and over which you had little if any control. At different times in the last few chapters, I've described *thriving* as a feeling of having "enough." Here, Malcolm describes a career as the feeling of being "full," even comparing arriving at a career to reaching the end of a buffet, having eaten one's fill of experiences during the course of a working life. This sense of fullness is Malcolm's way of talking about having enough in life.

The other thing that feels important to mention here is how the last conversation about career connects to and includes an element of time. This group is young, the oldest are only twenty-one years old, and while *job* and *work* feels proximate and close to their day-to-day experience, a career for most exists in the distance. Lyrik says "it's the last stop on the train," and Ali echoes this perspective, when he calls a career an "endgame." For Malcolm, Lyrik, Ali, Cedric and Xavier there is a finality to a career, a heaviness and gravity to it. They imagine that having reached a career; they will have arrived at a specific place or point in time in their lives—they frame it as the payoff for the *work* that they are doing now.

I want you to notice something else as well. The agency, the desire for and commitment to forward motion. When Lukas describes his mother's college degrees and his perception that her life has stagnated, he is also describing a desire to do something different by moving away from what he describes as just "nothing." And when in this last brief snippet, the group talks about what a career might be, they describe it in language that is almost oppositional to that of a job—it is something you do after doing other things, it is what you get to do or find for yourself after exploring, after trying things on and trying ideas out. There is an implicit expectation in Xavier's last statement—that a career is something that works for you—and if it doesn't, then it's something that you can change.

JOB, WORK, AND CAREER: SURVIVING, STRIVING, AND THRIVING

It is here that we begin to consider the middle state of the continuum and, indeed, the substance of an occupational pathway. The middle part of their journeys are where the plan is hatched and the effort made to move from where one currently stands to the place that one envisions one should be. For many in this group, this is a period in which one engages in work in order to move away from experiences of surviving and toward work experiences in which one feels they are thriving.

Now that you've gotten a foothold into the conversation, and are getting to know this group of young men, let's look at *striving*. What does it look like for this group of young men to set goals, plan for, and experience forward motion toward one's dreams and aspirations? Who and what do they expect to be of support as they chart their course, and what challenges do they imagine will stand in their way?

CHAPTER 3

What It Looks Like to Build Your Own Pathway

In the previous chapter, Xavier, Malcolm, Lamar, Cedric, Lyrik, Ali, and Lukas described the emotional and occupational states they associate with *surviving* and *thriving;* with *job,* and *career.* In this chapter we will move further into their conversation and focus on *striving* and *work;* we will begin to see how this group of young men were considering and constructing their respective journeys toward the "good lives" to which they aspired.

What did it look like for this group of young men to set goals, plan for, and experience forward motion toward their dreams and aspirations? *Striving* is the planning phase of an occupational pathway. *Striving* is characterized by identifying short- and long-term goals, making plans to achieve those goals, and adjusting as more information about oneself and the world dashes some plans and opens other opportunities. *Striving* should feel familiar to many of you who are reading this book. A great many interventions in education and career pathways spaces are focused on *striving:* Allowing students to receive college credit while enrolled in high school, connecting high school curricula more readily and clearly to labor market demands, and helping students plan for and identify post-secondary education opportunities. Of course, this focus makes sense—figuring out what goals to set and how to make progress toward them can be difficult well into one's adulthood.

Our research bears this out. Across focus groups, most young people aspired to live "good lives" and believed that they could and would achieve and experience a state of *thriving* at some point in their futures. Many young people also understood that some amount of hard work and effort would be necessary to reach their personal and career goals; in other words, they believed that some amount of *striving* would be necessary to experience *thriving*. However, when the moderator asked participants to articulate the specific experiences, skills, people, or information they might need to reach their goals, or what *striving* might look like in their own lives, many struggled.

In the New York group, as in many of the focus groups, the young men shared an orientation towards *thriving*. They imagined they would one day experience financial stability, own a home or business, travel when and where they wanted, give back to or support their parents and communities, and start and care for their own families. They also shared their experiences of *surviving*, when they were working or had worked *jobs* in which they had little or no control over their time, schedule, and labor, that they found boring or repetitive, and that they felt they had to do just to get by.

In exploring the notion of *striving*, we observed some important differences among the young men in the group. These differences reveal opportunities for adults to provide the support and resources young people will need to set and reach their life and career goals.

PATHWAY ARCHETYPES

Let's return to the pathway image. Though the pathways exercise only made up one part of the focus group time, it is a helpful anchor in the conversation about *striving*. The exercise enabled young people to describe their life plans and map out where they felt they were starting and the direction in which they wanted to move. As you listen to the participant's narrations of their pathway images and the discussion that follows, you can clearly see their goals, expectations for how their futures would unfold, the support they thought they might need, and the barriers they thought they might encounter. On one end, each participant wrote a career or life goal he wanted to achieve. He then placed himself on the path or off the path based on his own perspective of how far he had come and how far he needed to go to reach their stated goal. Finally, he wrote down the steps he imagined taking from where he felt he was now to where he wanted to be.

As my colleagues and I analyzed the pathway images across focus groups, we noted differences in how well-equipped young people felt to set goals for themselves and how confident they were that they either possessed or could locate the information, resources, and people they thought they might need to achieve their goals. We found these differences so notable that we created a framework, *Five Occupational Pathways*, to describe the different permutations of these confidences observed across pathways. The framework includes five archetypal pathways.

Pathway 1: *Know* what they want to do and *know* how to get there

Pathway 2: *Not sure* what they want to do, yet they *have a good idea* of the steps to take to explore to get there

Pathway 3: *Know* what they want to do, but they are *unsure* how to get there

Pathway 4: *Not sure* what they want to do and *unsure* of what steps to take

Pathway 5: *Know* what they want to do and *think they know* how to get there, but their imagined pathway is inaccurate and/or unrealistic

It can be tempting to use categories like these prescriptively—lumping the young people you know or work with into each. I want to caution against this. As an analytical tool, the framework helped us to make meaning from and distinguish between a large volume of pathway discussions and imagery. But every framework has shortcomings. I have come to believe that this one places too much weight on how adult researchers interpret the quality of young people's goals and aspirations and too little on the knowledge young people bring to designing their pathways. Just as the framework can be a way to understand where young people may need additional support, it can also be a way to understand the many ways that young people are exercising agency in their own lives by making informed decisions about what they want to learn, how they want to live and who they want to be.

STEPPING STONES

You may recall from chapter two that *striving* looks different for everyone. It is not surprising that young people understand the steps they will need to take to either form or reach their goals differently. Some young people are concerned with building personal and professional relationships; some are focused on emotional growth and self-regulation; and others feel that instructional knowledge, like earning degrees and certifications, will be the key to their success. In most cases, a pathway includes two or more types of steps: relational, emotional, and instructional.

While no single focus group provides a perfect example of all five pathways or every permutation of stepping stones, listening to the young men in New York will give you a sense of how young people's life experiences inform their aspirations and their plans, and the diversity of ways young people's pathways can be interpreted. In addition, I encourage you to take note of the emphasis this group of young men places on emotions, having and building relationships, and their perception that they are the most important agents of change in their lives, with the power to both catalyze movement toward and stand in the way of their goals. As in the last chapter, the text will alternate between shorter passages from a single speaker and longer dialogue in which the group discusses an idea raised in the conversation. Peppered throughout are my own observations and analyses, meant to connect the dots between what I've laid out above and the young people's own words and ideas.

YOUNG PEOPLE WHO KNOW WHAT THEY WANT TO DO AND KNOW HOW TO GET THERE

Xavier

Xavier was nineteen years old and had earned his GED. You have previously heard Xavier introduce himself, "My name is Xavier. I'm nineteen, and I work as a sales associate at GameStop. And I live with family." Xavier dreamt about becoming a gamer and described his thoughts on how he would achieve his goal to the group.

> XAVIER: *I'm starting out now working at GameStop and doing local tournaments and streaming. I went to a recent local tournament, and I got fourth place. After a few months, [I'm going to] become a Senior Game Associate (SGA), then become a manager.*
>
> *And then while I'm doing my tournaments and my streaming, hopefully, I get scouted by Echo Fox or Panda Global . . . and trained by Sonic Fox or Lothario. Then I would like to be . . . working with, a team. And then I want to become number one in whatever game I start to specialize in in the US, go to nationals, DreamHack, Evo, or SummerSlam. And then last, I would like to become a trainer or manage my own team.*
>
> *Basically, I want to be scouted by two of the biggest eSport teams. And then I want to be trained by their top players. And then I want to become number one in the US in whatever game I decide to play. Then I want to hit nationals and*

WHAT IT LOOKS LIKE TO BUILD YOUR OWN PATHWAY   55

FIGURE 3.1   Xavier's Pathway Image

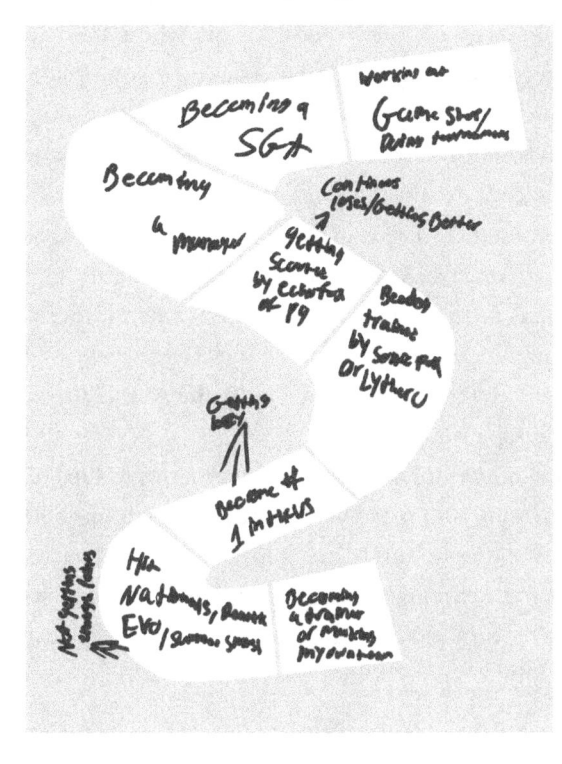

Name: Xavier	Become #1 in the US
Top to bottom	H12 Nationals, DreamHack EVO/Summer Smash
Path: Working at Game Stop/ Doing tournaments	
Becoming a SGA	Becoming a trainer or making my own team
Becoming a manager	**Outside path:** Continues loses/Getting Better
Getting scouted by echofox or PG	Getting lazy
Being trained by Sonic Fox or Lythero	Not getting enough points

the rest of the biggest gaming tournaments of the year. And then I want to become a trainer for the team that I decide to be on. Or I want to become a manager of my own. It could be anywhere from literally now to twenty years from now because, after the age of twenty-one, you're technically too old for eSports.

ALI: *You're too old after twenty-one?*

XAVIER: *You're too old after twenty-one.*

MALCOLM: *So only twenty-one-year-olds play their video games?*

XAVIER: *If you're not scouted by the age of twenty-one, your [chances] go down slowly because technically, your brain actually stops developing, and you actually start getting slower after the age of twenty-one.*

MALCOLM: *I think that's a crock of bull crap. But I see them things happening for you, brother.*

I have shared this dialogue excerpt to note a few things. First, I can see how easy it would be for someone to discount Xavier's dream of becoming a gamer.

In our initial coding of these pathways, we missed it too—describing this pathway as a "young person who knows what they want to do but whose steps are unrealistic." This initial categorization was a reflection of our own assumptions about the types of careers and work that were achievable and what dreams seemed attainable. When rereading the transcript, I could see Xavier's plan more clearly. I noticed the choices he'd already made that kept him proximate to gaming and the gaming community: his job at GameStop and his participation in local and regional tournaments. Xavier was also iterating on his goal and the steps to reach his goal as he received and was exposed to new information, such as the factoid about brain development plateauing at age twenty-one. Listening to Xavier in this new way led me to recode his pathway and altered my perception of his goals and aspirations.

Second, Xavier had created other supports to help him progress toward his goals. He had found his chosen family—a friend who pushed him to think about his interests as a potential career pathway. This friend motivated Xavier to pursue his dream of becoming a trainer and encouraged him by identifying steps and opportunities that could help him learn more about himself and refine his goals and his steps.

XAVIER: *I think the only person that inspired me to like actually pursue what I wanted to do is my ex-roommate. Because I was actually really tired of living with my parents. At the age of 16, I moved out. And I started living with him. And then he pushed me to actually get better at what I was doing with gaming. He was like why don't you turn it into your career if you love it so much? Because he streams as well . . . And he's been pushing his followers and using the clips I've had from my games and puts it on his Facebook and his YouTube and his Instagram. And now I slowly am getting, like, my following.*

In Xavier's pathway image, you can see how he prioritized the people, information, and resources that make up the gaming world. He worked at Gamestop, a place where he had access to gaming supplies and tournaments and where he could be close to the core business of gaming. He constructed the milestones of his journey around making and building relationships within the gaming community—by getting scouted, getting trained, and becoming a coach himself. It seemed possible, even likely, that his early experience and success at building non-familial supportive relationships with his friend and roommate led him to believe relationships could be opportunities in his path.

Cedric

Cedric's choices for his pathway progression looked and sounded different from Xavier's—but could also be assigned to the same pathway archetype, "knows what they want to do, and knows how to get there." Cedric's path is perhaps more recognizable to those of us who work to improve education and career pathways. Cedric has already begun a professional certification while still in high school. As seen previously, Cedric was seventeen and introduced himself saying, "Hi, my name is Cedric. I work at Burger King. And I live with my mom and my dad and my brother." He described his pathway in the following way:

CEDRIC: *Right now. I'm a high school . . . senior, working at Burger King, college undecided, working. I'm trying to build up my money to move out of my mom's house. And then buy my own place [and] all of that. I don't know what else. That's really it. I'm going to do HVAC [*Heating, Ventilation, and Air Conditioning*] if I do go to college . . . my teacher told me I could make $40,000 more if I go to college [*for two years*].*

MALCOLM: *So don't you want to make that $40,000 more?*

CEDRIC: *I go to a program and I do HVAC there. I was doing that since last year. It's my second year, so I get my certification this year.*

MALCOLM: *Congratulations brother. Nice, that's lit.*

LAMAR: *That's what's up.*

MALCOLM: *They need more Black people like you out there in the world.*

CEDRIC: *Thank you.*

While some group members used the pathway exercise to write out their future plans, others wrote little to nothing on the image. Instead, these individuals, like Cedric, seemed to use the pathway activity as more of a prompt for what they shared verbally with the group. Cedric's narration of his path included a series of instructional and technical steps centered on getting his professional certification in HVAC and then getting to work. While many of the young people in this group viewed high school and even college as something they had to do—having little or nothing to do with their career pathway, Cedric, made a direct

58 HOW WE SEE US

FIGURE 3.2 Cedric's Pathway Image

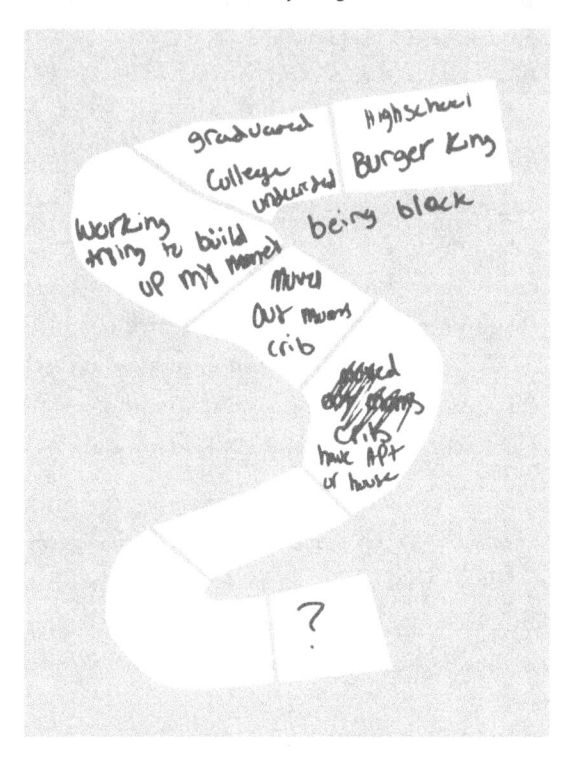

Name: Cedric	up my money
	Move
Top to bottom	Out Moms crib
Path: High school Burger King	~~Moved~~ ~~Out Moms~~ ~~crib~~ have Apt or house
graduated College undecided	?
Working trying to build	**Outside path:** being black

connection between school and career, saying at one point in the conversation that even though he doesn't like school, it still feels like something you do to further your career.

MODERATOR: *What feels like the opposite of a "good job?"*
CEDRIC: *School. I hate my school.*
XAVIER: *Waking up every morning like fuck I got to go to this shit.*
CEDRIC: *Waking up every morning that's the worst . . . having to get to school on time, going to all of my classes, and getting out, and going to work, it's stressful.*
MODERATOR: *What makes school feel like a bad job?*
CEDRIC: *I mean, because you still got to [do it], to graduate, so that's a job. You better do it to further your career.*

Interestingly, Cedric's written pathway does not mention the HVAC certificate. Looking at his pathway image, you can see that he left several spaces blank, even ending the pathway with a question mark. Instead of steps toward a career,

Cedric's written pathway focused on a series of milestones connected to experiencing financial independence. For example, his pathway includes the steps of "moving out of mom's crib" and "working, trying to build up my money," and the furthest of his steps focuses not on what he will do for work but *how* he wants to live. Having "an apartment or a house" functions as a proxy for what it will feel like when he achieves his unnamed goal. It is only when the group is asked how they imagine their lives at ages twenty-five and seventy and how they imagine their day-to-day experience that Cedric returned to the HVAC certificate and career goals. When he imagined his life in eight years at age twenty-five, he said,

CEDRIC: *I see myself doing HVAC. That's heating, insulation, air conditioning . . . So I see myself doing that still in New York until I get enough money to move . . . somewhere down South, it's cheaper down there.*

After the group discussed the opportunities and dangers of moving "down South," Cedric said that Atlanta might be a good place to start a business. By the time he reached seventy, he wanted to be retired from working, living in Florida or "somewhere hot," but with a business model that still allowed him to earn some money from his HVAC business.

On the one hand, Cedric's oral description of his pathway focused on the details and milestones of his career trajectory in HVAC. He was in school and working towards a professional certification; he was motivated to consider going to college to increase his earnings, and he could articulate what it could be like to start out as an HVAC technician and progress to owning his own business. On the other hand, Cedric's written pathway was firmly rooted in the quality of life a career in HVAC could provide, namely increased financial independence. It is difficult to discern whether Cedric interpreted the exercise differently than other members of this focus group or if he intended the two pathways (oral and written) to be complementary, where one described his instructional steps and the other the emotional experience of completing the steps. I see the two pathways as complementary, with the steps necessary to pursue a career existing in parallel to, but separate from, what it will feel like to live the life that a career enables.

Lamar

Twenty-year-old Lamar also had a concrete career goal and a clear sense of what he needed to do to reach it. Remember, Lamar wanted to be a working actor and was already taking acting classes and auditioning for small roles in television shows. Lamar was the first in the group to frame the *job* he works for money as secondary to the *work* he does to pursue his career. In chapter 2 it is Lamar who says, "The moment we clock out, that's when it becomes, all right, it's work. We're working on our own, you know, personal goals." In Lamar, I see a highly organized young person who is actively searching for and finding the information he needs to make the decisions and take the steps that will help him achieve his career goals. Describing his pathway Lamar says,

LAMAR: *Mine is a little different because I kind of... touched like small things on it so far. But, first one I put, you know, I'm working at a job, and I'm in acting classes. Second thing is auditioning and building a resume. Third thing for me is practicing self tape.[1] So basically, that's setting your core self in whatever scene you're doing.*

The next one after that is background jobs. So I have like a couple background jobs on like Law and Order and stuff like that. After that, it's principal roles. That's when you see the people that have like one line on TV shows. After that for me, you'll be signed to an agency. Like two summers ago, I had this audition where it was for a human trafficking show. I actually got picked up for it. They're still in preproduction. But if things go good, it's going to Netflix. And then after that, I'm officially a working actor.

Do you have an extra sheet? Because I want to actually like take this [gestures at his completed pathway image] home . . . just keep it to like, this is what we got to do.

Lamar, perhaps more than the others in this chapter, conceived of the pathway image as a plan. He used the exercise to map out and sequence the various aspects of a working actor's life: going to auditions, preparing self-tapes, and getting an agent. In explaining to the group where he was in relationship to his end goal, he said he's already touched "small things" on his path, making it clear that he saw himself as someone capable of progressing toward his goal. Lamar ended the narration of his pathway by asking to take the image home so that he can remember what he wrote down and what he has to do to become a working actor. For Lamar there was something powerful about writing his plan and sharing it with the group: a transformative aspect of the focus group and the exercise. In chapter 4, I discuss this unintended but welcome impact of the focus group in greater detail.

WHAT IT LOOKS LIKE TO BUILD YOUR OWN PATHWAY   61

FIGURE 3.3   Lamar's Pathway Image

Name:
LAMAR

Top to Bottom

any job
audition
Acting classes

[Outside with arrow – accept who I am and what I cant change]

audition
building resume

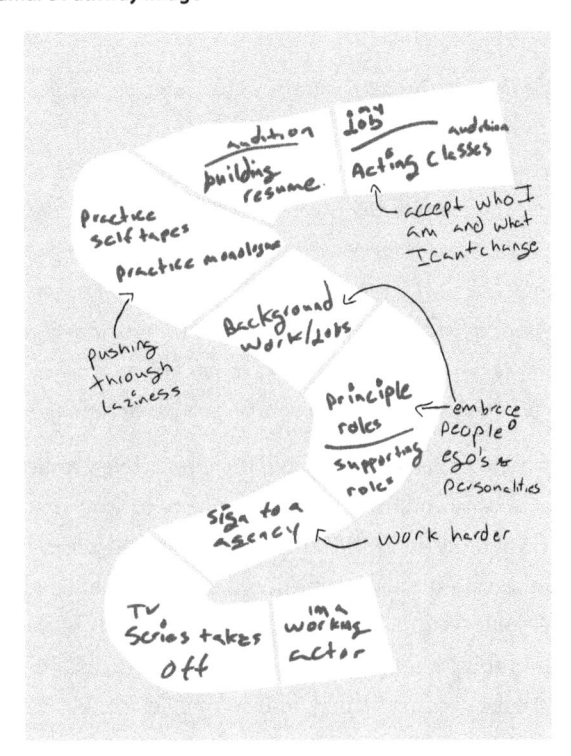

Practice self tapes
Practice monologues

[Outside with arrow – pushing through laziness]

Background work/jobs

Principle roles
Supporting roles

[Outside with arrows connecting to Background work/jobs and Principle roles

supporting roles – embrace people ego's & personalities]

Sign to a agency

[Outside with arrow – work harder]

TV series takes off

im a working actor

While his initial description of his career pathway was focused mostly on procedural steps, Lamar also seemed to recognize the importance of relationships and community in his path. At various points in the conversation, he described his efforts to build relationships with casting agents, directors, and fellow creatives to remain connected to the industry and to acting. While optimistic that he could reach his goal, Lamar appeared clear-headed about the difficulties he may encounter pursuing his career goals.

LAMAR: *I feel like the negative with acting . . . you're going to different directors who are constantly telling you no, no, no.*

So for people who think . . . it's a walk in the park, it's like, no, you got to wake up every day knowing that you're going to get rejected. But that one time that a director or a casting director could be like, no, he might have something, that's when it becomes, all right, so all of my hard work paid off for something. You know, that's the sense of relief you can get at the end of the day. But if you don't have the thick skin, you're just too dark, or you're too tall, or you're too skinny, or you ain't big enough. So that's when it becomes, like, you got to be tough.

When I step back, Lamar's pathway and his approach feel realistic. He will learn more about what being a working actor entails as he participates in the work of being an actor. Lamar is making plans and setting near-term and longer-term goals, while also seeking out the exposure and experiences that will help him to further refine his pathway and his goal. We can see in Lamar's pathway a mix of the stepping stones described earlier in this chapter: taking acting classes (instructional), building professional relationships (relational), and developing a "thick skin" (emotional).

YOUNG PEOPLE WHO ARE NOT SURE WHAT THEY WANT TO DO, YET THEY HAVE A GOOD IDEA OF THE STEPS TO TAKE TO EXPLORE TO GET THERE

Lukas

In contrast to the specificity of Cedric, Xavier, and Lamar's pathways, Lukas did not have a specific career goal toward which he was working. Instead, Lukas was focused on emotional and personal growth. Lukas' path was dominated by efforts to change and redefine himself. He spoke about himself in terms that led me to believe he was making a conscious effort to transform himself and his outlook, all while building or strengthening the qualities that he believed were essential to eventually setting more specific goals and attaining his notion of a "good life."

Most immediately, Lukas seemed concerned with rejecting where he had come from and embracing his chosen family and his new city: New York. In the last chapter, Lukas grappled with the value of college and rejected the unhappiness he saw in the family members whose education and career choices had led them to "just working just to work." He continued by saying, "They went to school.

WHAT IT LOOKS LIKE TO BUILD YOUR OWN PATHWAY   63

FIGURE 3.4   Lukas' Pathway Image

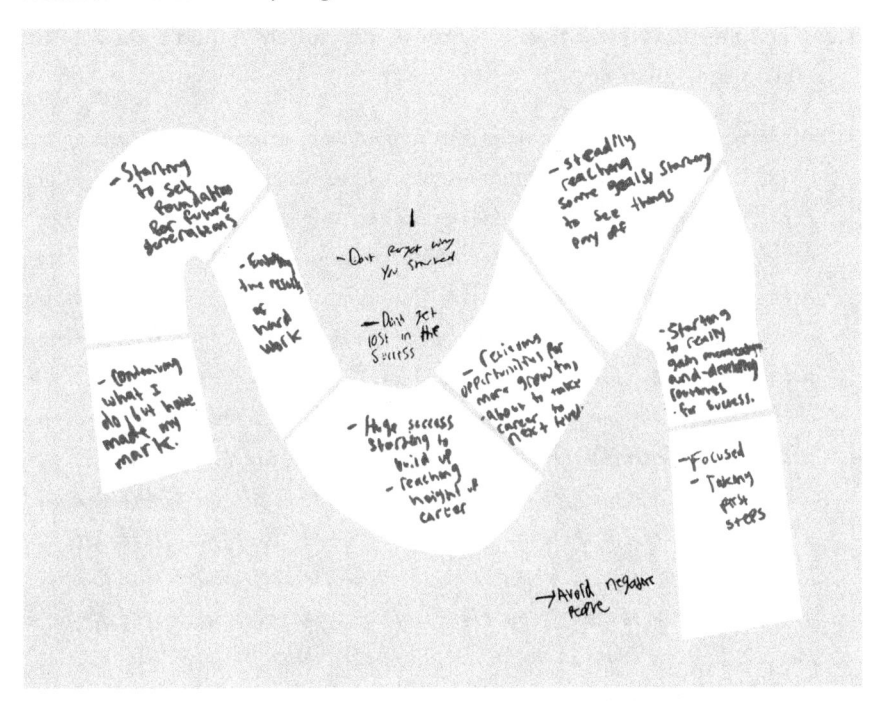

Name: Lukas

Top to bottom

Path:
-Focused
-Taking first steps

-starting to really gain momentum and developing routines for success.

-steadily reaching some goals, starting to see things pay off

-recieving opportunities for more growth,
-about to take career to next level

-Huge success starting to build up

-reaching height of career

-Enjoy the rewards of hard work

-Starting to set foundation for future generations

-Continuing what I do but have made my mark.

Outside path:
-Dont forget why you started
-Dont get lost in the success

→Avoid negative People

They have master's, you know, or bachelor's or whatever. But they're not working in their field. So I know they're not happy. They tell me they're not happy. I see it on their face." Lukas felt his family members had too readily believed that going to college and acquiring degrees was the key to attaining a "good life." When Lukas spoke about his family, you had the sense he didn't want to be taken advantage of or swindled in the same way. In rejection of these instructional steps, he framed his own career pathway almost entirely around emotional and relational steps. Lukas described his pathway,

LUKAS: *Well, right now . . . I'm more conscious and aware than ever this year specifically in . . . what I really want to do, [what] I'm passionate about. So right now [I'm] planning, goal setting, and then [*the next step is*] work consistency, network building, and adding to my skills and my natural abilities. And then next would be . . . when the opportunity comes to accumulate my wealth from that and stay mindful, like, humble. [I'll] remember what I'm really going for. If given the opportunity, I'll be exposed to, you know, a lot of powerful and successful people like the hierarchy of the world. And then . . . I'll try to learn as much as I can from just observing and learning through my mistakes and growing through that. Working more than ever and like, you know, more consistently, harder, and more dedicated, and travel the world, hopefully through my work. Then from there, after . . . being exposed to so many successful, powerful people, then make a plan to run my own business and to own my own land, and . . . own everything in my life for me and for the generations in my family to be passed down.*

*After I, you know, start owning and getting my stuff together for, you know, to stabilize myself and my family, I'll travel the world . . . probably live everywhere for like a month, and give back to local businesses, to families in the communities, and see . . . who needs help, and cater to them. And then after I go on that whole . . . humanitarian tour . . . I'll be more stabilized through my work. And I'll be more known. And I'll have like a steady supply of [*clients.*] And then the end goal is just fulfillment, success, wealth, enjoyment.*

What will he do? What kind of business will he run? For Lukas, his career goal was still unknown to him. He knew he wanted to do something that allowed him to own a business and land, to travel, to "stabilize," and to pass down wealth. He focused on the emotional quality of the steps and the feeling he hoped to have as he progressed through them. He wanted to strengthen his "natural abilities" and "build skills"—ideas core to occupational identity (what you are good at and the skills you believe you have), even while having very little clarity about what he was building towards.

Like Xavier, Lukas believed connecting to people doing work that interested him would be an important part of his pathway and that through these "networks," he would gain access to new information that would, in turn, inform his thinking about his goals and his steps. When asked about the role of "networks" in his pathway, Lukas says:

LUKAS: *It's just in me being around those people, you know, that's the opportunity to learn from them and to, you know, if you want what somebody else has, be around them, learn from them, learn what you can take from them, and apply it to yourself.*

Early on, Lukas told the group that his family didn't have his back. Part of Lukas' journey had already involved leaving his family's home, and, like Xavier, Lukas had found a family of chosen peers who could support him. Lukas believed that he would need other people to move forward on his path. However, he did not describe how he anticipated meeting these people. This was common across focus groups, where young people knew relationships could provide necessary support but felt unsure about how to build or cultivate them.

When I introduced the pathways archetypes at the beginning of this chapter, I cautioned against applying them prescriptively. There are at least two different ways to interpret Lukas' pathway. One perspective is that while Lukas may not have a clear goal, his strong focus on emotional and personal growth indicates he understands some of the foundational steps needed to explore his future options and make progress along his path. This interpretation assigns some value to his interest in personal development and his awareness that he will need to build and attend to his self-confidence in order to figure out how he wants to live and what he wants to do for a career.

Alternatively, Lukas' pathway might reflect his profound uncertainty. Without defined education and career-development steps or an actionable plan, he appears unsure about his goals and the path to achieving them. Emphasizing this aspect of his pathway, one might assign Lukas to a different pathway archetype: *Young people who are not sure what they want to do and unsure of what steps to take.* Either interpretation reveals opportunities for support and guidance.

The pathway archetypes can help us identify and understand what young people *don't know* and what young people *do know*, and perhaps more importantly, how they are making informed decisions about their lives. In this chapter, Xavier, Cedric, Lamar, and Lukas *know* a lot about what they want to experience when they reach their goals. They *do know* what they aspire to feel, even if they *don't know* what profession will enable them to feel this way. They *do know* and understand the value of effort, struggle, relationships, persistence, and self-reliance. Too often, we overlook the knowledge young people bring to decision-making about education and careers. Instead of recognizing young people, like the young men in New York, as experts in the messiness of *striving*, we cast them as immature, directionless, under-prepared novices making ill-informed decisions that will have irreversible impacts on their future lives.[2] This makes it easy to see how a deficit narrative emerges.

Striving, like adolescence, is rarely neat and orderly. It is full of gathering and making meaning of the information, resources, people, and experiences that are available and simultaneously trying to figure out how to put that information to use. *Striving* is a time during which young people are shaping and articulating dreams and goals and, sometimes for the first time, taking responsibility for reaching them.[3] It is only in hindsight that the choices, detours, and mistakes that we make as adolescents become part of a more cohesive story we tell as adults about our own agency, self-efficacy, or luck. So, too, is the case with *striving*. It is only in reflecting that we draw a direct connection between the career, family, and life we have as older adults and the choices we make in our youth and young adulthood. We have an obligation to recognize the insights and experiences young people possess as valuable knowledge that informs the decisions they make about education and careers. Far from disregarding what young men like Lyrik, Xavier, Cedric, and Lamar have already learned about themselves and how the world works, our role as supportive adults should be to notice what they *know* and then meet them where they are by sharing the information, relationships, exposure, and experiences that can increase the quality of the decisions they are already making.

THE CHALLENGES AND BARRIERS THAT STAND IN THE WAY

As you look at the pathway images in the previous pages, you may notice words or scribbles in the margins. After each person completed the steps of their pathway, I asked them to write down and then discuss the events and people that might help them to reach their goals and also those that might stand in the way. While many of the supports young people described have already been discussed in this chapter, the barriers have not. Across this group's pathway images and discussions, three categories of barriers emerged: those related to oneself, those related to one's lack of money or financial stability, and those related to society.

The first category: the self. To a person, one can see some variation of "myself" scrawled somewhere on the image or uttered in response. In our analysis, we created a shorthand for this: young people saw their success or failure as "all up to them." Think of Lyrik, who says the greatest barrier to his success is "my own negativity" and having small dreams; or Xavier, who says his own "laziness" and inability to learn from his mistakes could impede his success. In both cases, the young men place the notion of obstacles squarely within themselves. When asked how he might overcome the challenge of negativity, Lyrik said that he will have to work harder to be positive, but he doesn't say how he will do this or what actions he can take. Similarly, Xavier also is quiet when asked how he might overcome the laziness he feels might stand in his way.

The second category: financial concerns. In this group, several of the young men aspired to be entrepreneurs. They saw this as a way of avoiding the negative aspects of the *jobs* they held, making them their own bosses with control over their time and labor. Though less present in the pathway images, several young men spoke about the choice to be an entrepreneur or an actor in the case of Lamar, as requiring some financial and personal risk. They worried that they might run out of money before their dreams became a reality.

LUKAS: . . . *like one of the challenges I guess is going to be taking financial risk. Like, you know, when you own your own business, and you're really going for yourself, you have to sometimes take a risk and go out there. You know, hope for the best that it'll come back to you in return tenfold.*

ALI: *I think that, like, if you start your own business and stuff, you have to make sure you take responsibility for the people that work for you . . . because you're like you're the leader. You're responsible now. You have to take that responsibility. Some people don't want to do that. So they might, you know, be scared to like take that step.*

The third category: societal concerns. How external realities, in particular racism and discrimination, might impact their sense of possibility and their ability to make progress. Since assumptions about identity (the self) and structural inequality (societal concerns) drive many of the interventions and investments to improve career pathways for young people, it feels important to unpack how group members spoke about their identities—broadly and also in terms of race and gender—and also how they engaged with issues of racism and discrimination.

PERCEPTIONS OF SELF AND IDENTITY

Early in the discussion, I asked the participants to write on a sheet of paper a list of words and phrases they would use to describe themselves and, secondarily, to write a list of words and phrases they would use to describe their backgrounds, with a sub prompt inviting them to include their race, gender, religion, community, culture, and other aspects of their backgrounds. The first list included words and phrases that were mostly positive and focused almost exclusively on their familial relationships, personality traits, and their role in activities they were good at or cared about. For example, some young people described themselves in terms of their familial relationships, and others in terms of their personalities and behaviors. The second list describing backgrounds was more matter-of-fact and neutral, often describing race, gender, and religion. After writing down their list of words, they were asked to share them with the group. Here are some of the ways young people described themselves.

CEDRIC: Tall, hardworking, humble, fast, athletic, Black male

LUKAS: Hardworking, self-sufficient, empathetic, mindful, peaceful, patient, curious, reader, humorous

LAMAR: Dreamer, motivated, passionate, over-thinker, and humble

XAVIER: Male, African American, spiritual, but nonreligious

MALCOLM: Black, gay Baptist, stylist

Overwhelmingly, the group described themselves in positive or neutral terms. This positivity is consistent with their optimism about their abilities to reach their goals. They talked about themselves and their identities mostly as assets they brought to their work, dreams, and aspirations. Throughout the conversation we can see how Lamar's description of himself as "motivated" and a "dreamer" is present in his description of his plan to become an actor. Or how Lukas' description of himself as mindful, self-sufficient, and empathetic connects to how he centers his own emotions in this pathway. I raise this asset framing around identity before moving into the discussion about racism because I think it is important to notice that without the context of education and career, many Black young people, including this group in New York, saw their identity, and in particular their race, as a neutral characteristic in their lives. This is another reminder that the framing and narrative we apply to young people is often not the narrative they apply to themselves.

In fact, in this group of young men who shared the same racial identity, oppression, and unfair treatment because of their race and gender were not particularly central to the two-hour conversation. As a reader, depending on the community you come from and the experiences and assumptions you bring to this book, that may be easier or harder to believe. In this group, concerns about racism emerged at only two points in the discussion. The first was fairly early on when I asked the group to consider what their lives might look like at age twenty-five.

MODERATOR: Okay, what's important to you at twenty-five?
LYRIK: *Twenty-five? Making it to twenty-six.*
MALCOLM: *I hear that.*
XAVIER: *No, that's real.*
LAMAR: *That's a fact.*

You might notice in the excerpt above that race is subtext. Lyrik doesn't say explicitly he is worried about making it to twenty-six because of racism or discrimination, but it is implied. The second time the group discusses racism is when I ask the group directly how they anticipate their self-described racial and gender identities will impact or influence their education and career goals:

ALI: *Like, I feel like . . . obviously there will be like people that will try to hold you back. But like at the end of the day, you still got to put in that work. Yeah, he's white. He's probably going to get the job before you, but what are you going to do about it? Like are you just going, okay, I'm not going to do it then? You got to work harder. I think you definitely got to work harder as a Black man or a woman in general just to like get your spot because that's just the way it is right now.*

MALCOLM: *. . . being Black is already hard. To be gay on top of that is ten times harder than that because I'm telling right now, they just already think you're less of what, less of a man or less of anything. And I ain't none of those, just know that. So it's kind of like you got to prove yourself ten times more just to be noticed. So I just, like I said, I just try to always, I try to start everything out with a joke. I feel like that's always the best way to do things for me. I've learned that, for me, it just makes things easier. Try to make everybody laugh in the situation, try to just be a frontrunner, try not to be, that's why I'm so loud and rambunctious.*

LYRIK: *Oh, like he said, you got to start everything with a joke. Like people in school be like, Lyrik, why you never serious? Because if you get serious, we all going to be sitting here crying.*

XAVIER: *Yeah . . . I don't like being serious.*

LAMAR: *Yeah, and I think . . . there's just 24 hours in a day. There's so much going on in this world. We need something to laugh at, you know . . . because if not, we'll, like he said, we'll kind of be . . . uptight about everything. Like, you know, we're Black. We get it. We know there's a target on our back. We know that. But if we don't embrace life for what it is, we just going to be focused on, oh, they out to get me. And this is going to be hard. So we got to like kind of just kind of numb the pain, take life for what it is, laugh about it, and work hard for it, move past it.*

Moments like these can be interpreted in many different ways. Some of our project advisors were surprised by how this part of the conversation unfolded, stating that this response—a conscious or subconscious unwillingness to treat their reality as a landmine—was a product of trauma. Advisors, with decades of experience working in the youth and career development fields, worried that these young people were either ignorant of or choosing to ignore the magnitude at which discrimination and racial bias might disrupt their journey toward their goals.

I see it differently. I see this as an exchange between young Black men who are acknowledging what they believe to be a shared, albeit unfair reality, and are recognizing one another's experiences as honest and real. In their statements Xavier, Lyrik, Malcolm, Ali, and Lamar treat racism as a fact of life: not something to be fixed but something to be overcome. I want to point out something you can't see by reading the text: the group's physical reaction to the question itself and a change of the mood in the room.

Up until that point, the conversation had been increasingly driven by the young men at the table. But I was the one who asked them to think about the impact of their race and gender on education, career, and work, and, in doing so, I unintentionally suggested that it could be a barrier. Something shifted in the room, and I felt as though my question had intruded on their conversation. The group had been looking at one another, engaged in one another's words—they had established a flow. My interjection seemed to take them out of their discussion. They looked at each other and then at me. There seemed to be a collective fatigue and perhaps boredom with this line of questioning. It was palpable, like, "Of course, *you* want to talk about that—everyone wants to talk about that."

Perhaps it is this fatigue in the second exchange that prompts the group not to spend a lot of time talking about the instances of racism they had already experienced or expected to experience. Instead, they moved almost immediately to what it would take to overcome racism: hard work and developing coping mechanisms like laughter to keep tears at bay. I used epistemic network analysis (ENA), "a method for identifying and quantifying connections among elements in coded data," to map and then measure the connections between participants and to compare the structure and the strength of associations between themes of identity, discrimination, career, and work.[4] ENA allowed me to see that the early conversation about identity, race, background, and gender, devoid of all mention of career and education, was mostly positive. A shift occurred when the group talked about these aspects of their identities in the contexts of *career* and *work*. In other words, context mattered. I can't help but wonder if some small part of this shift was due to the deficit narratives about Black young men and work that are pervasive in our society and to which they had likely already been exposed. And I wondered, then and now, what it would look like if we reinforced the notion that part of our work as change-makers and those who seek to improve education and career pathways requires that we help young people to carry within themselves positive narratives that they can call upon to resist deficit narratives. What would it look like if we focused some of our attention on the narratives and the sources of the narratives that are causing harm?

DISRUPTING MYTHS ABOUT PATHWAYS TO CAREER

As we approach the end of this chapter and our time with the young men in New York, I want to highlight a few more observations. The first concerns the notion of a pathway to career as a linear progression. In New York, only Lyrik and Cedric alluded to the possibility that they may one day change their minds and need to adjust their expectations and aspirations or pivot. Lyrik wrote on his pathway that he might "make a mistake" early on and have to learn from it and make a new choice. Cedric said he was still figuring out if it made sense for him to go to college—admitting that choosing not to go right away didn't prohibit him from going at some later point in the future. The other young people in this chapter seemed to conceive of their future plans as somewhat of a straight line.

One step or decision stacked on the last, with little or no indication that their desires, needs, or interests might change over time. Admittedly, this preference for linearity may be partly due to the nature of the exercise. The pathway image could have reinforced the idea of moving from one end to the other, from point A to point B. Perhaps we would have seen more feedback loops, more on-ramps, and off-ramps if the image had been drawn differently. Regardless of why the resulting images looked the way they did, the discussion around paths to and through education and career suggested that there would be few opportunities to change one's mind, to consider new information, or to refine one's plan. How could this be?

Part of the answer might lie in the stories we tell about the transitions from K–12 to post-secondary education, career, and work, and relatedly the narratives we hold about how careers are arrived at and how much agency we have in determining what we do for work. Many of us subscribe—consciously or subconsciously—to the idea of "making it." Despite data that suggests American adults change careers several times and a proliferation of recruitment, upskilling, and job training solutions to meet this need, many young people understand a career as a one-time permanent decision: a choice one makes once and then lives with forever.[5] In other words, we talk about getting a "good job" and the markers of a "good life" as being both obviously defined and also fixed. But this is far from the truth. If we are lucky, we are always innovating and uncovering a more authentic good life; we are always re-equipping ourselves to make that new and better decision, whether we force it into being or it arrives on its own. We are also just as likely to make changes and be forced to or choose to pivot.

Reflect on your own life experience. Likely, the path to the city you live in, the field you work in, and the partner you chose was neither straight nor straightforward. I don't think we do enough to acknowledge this nonlinearity. Instead of emphasizing the challenges inherent in *striving*, we tell stories about young people who enter their career pathway as adolescents, living at home, living for the first time on their own, working or studying, doing both or doing neither—and then magically, and usually described as only a few steps later, they find themselves inexplicably independent, fully-fledged adults.

In talking too little about *striving*, we do young people a disservice. At the start, we prevent them from truly envisioning what this time could look like, or how the choices they make, the steps and experiences they take or have, and the people who come into their lives and those they seek out, will inform and sometimes change the direction of their paths. Young adults don't need to make choices for what they'll be doing when they're thirty-five; they need, when they're seventeen or eighteen or twenty-one, to be equipped to reflect on the experiences they've had so far and to see what those experiences teach them about who they are, what they are good at, and yes, where they feel they belong. We need to normalize that life and career pathways are full of feedback loops, starting over, mistakes, and detours. We need to normalize the messiness of *striving* and not require young people to make premature decisions about what education or career to pursue purely because we fear what might happen to them if they don't.

At the beginning of chapter 2, I shared why I chose to focus on young Black men: their stories are often curated in such a way as to justify what interventions are made and are, therefore, thin interpretations of their lives. Now, you may wonder why, within this demographic, I chose to focus on this discussion in New York—a group that is not full of aspiring engineers, physical therapists, army medics, or any number of other careers young people in the research saw themselves having. I chose this group because their imagined futures may sit at what I imagine is the very edges of our ability to hold the tension between what young people know about themselves and what we as adults know about the world. It is uncomfortable to consider the choice not to enroll in post-secondary education as being an informed one. It is uncomfortable to treat the dream of becoming an actor or a gamer with the same deference and seriousness we treat the HVAC technician, the radiologist, or the aspiring nurse. But I hope after reading this chapter, you can see that for young people who participated in this conversation, one dream is no more or less real than the others. In dreaming and imagining how their futures will play out, they are trusting us to see them as they see themselves. They are showing us something about what they have learned about themselves, what they understand to be true about their own abilities, their own skills, and what they feel they are good at. It is here that our work should begin, recognizing all that they know and all that they have already chosen and connecting our work to their own. And when we feel the noise of our immense expertise and decades of experience creeping in, making the space in our heads and our hearts almost too loud to listen, this is when we should lean closer. Find the thread, acknowledge young people's own brilliance, and lean in. Here, again, are the words of the young men in New York, describing how they imagine it will look and feel to *thrive*.

MODERATOR: Imagine that you're forty-five. What's your life like?

MALCOLM: *You know, I think I live in Spain. Yeah, I'm over all of this dang cold. It's either Spain, Barcelona, one of them places over there, you know, two kids, maybe three living it up, happy, family. I got my own business.*

XAVIER: *He's got his own line now.*

MALCOLM: *At forty-five, I really work as much as I want, so I guess I can say if I want to work 9:00 to 5:00, I work 9:00 to 5:00, so I can be home for the kids afterwards. If I want to work later at night, so I can be home throughout the day to take them to school, you know, it just depends on how I feel. So I can say anywhere between thirty-five to forty hours, you know, just regular hours, but just obviously, because I'm the boss, I can make or break those hours if I want to.*

MILES: *Man, that's deep.*

LAMAR: *I think at forty-five, after I've had my fun and did all of, you know, the things I wanted to do in terms of like with film and all of that, I would probably like open up an acting school, go back to the community, and find some acting students, inspire, like I want to take them, show them some things, train them, and then give them the dream and joy I had when I was they age, you know.*

MODERATOR: Okay. Ali, what about you, what's forty-five look like?

ALI: *I'll probably be chilling. I mean, hopefully, I have a good job, but, like, I don't want to be, like, working for somebody else because, like, that sucks. I want to have kind of like my own business idea or something. So that, like, what he said, like, I can be flexible with, like, what I want to do, like, how much I want to work.*

For some of you the framing of this book may feel problematic. You may object to my decision to privilege the futures that young people see for themselves over a laundry list of negative outcomes. To be clear, all of the research that tells us that the world may not meet their optimism with the respect and deference they deserve is also important. But this book is not about how researchers, academics, educators, policy makers, and philanthropists see young people who are Black and Hispanic; it is a book about how they see themselves. I suppose I'm putting a stake in the ground and saying that I feel I have little choice but to embrace the perspectives of Black and Hispanic young people on their own realities, given how inadequately they are represented in the spaces where adults like me talk about and ostensibly support the futures that young people want for themselves.

If we start to design our policies, programs, initiatives, and funding streams based on how young people see themselves, our goals become that much clearer. All of us engaged in the work of raising and supporting young people should be concerned with facilitating the exposure, experiences, and confidence they will need to make the very best decisions they can for themselves so that they can reach their dreams.

I hope this conversation among the young men in New York gave you a sense of what I felt and heard as I sat in the room. I heard optimism. I heard resilience. I also heard uncertainty about things not yet figured out and struggles already experienced. When considering young people's futures, nothing I've done since this project has shown me that we're doing any better at combating crisis narratives—or at fighting for young people's positivity and resilience and supporting them in decisions and choices not in prescribed pathways.

I have come to the conclusion that the solutions lie within giving more young people a chance to speak, to be in community with one another, and for us adults to listen to their conversations differently while keeping our worst fears for them at bay.

CHAPTER 4

Conversation as Intervention

One critique of research conducted with young people, particularly young people color, is that it can be extractive.[1] Focus groups are often designed to collect information about problems that have been defined by people with little or no shared experience with the young people who are researched. Researchers, often white, determine what knowledge is valuable and novel and, ultimately, what knowledge is worthy of sharing (i.e., disseminating) more broadly. Sometimes, young people aren't even compensated for their time, thoughts and insights. You can quickly see how research can have a way of perpetuating power imbalances.

In the previous three chapters, I've alternated between sharing verbatim quotes from the focus group discussions, analytical frameworks emergent from the research, and my own observations and reflections. I have tried to balance the importance of sharing the voices of individual young people with presenting and discussing findings that relate to, and provide insight into, how young people experience education and career pathways. In this chapter, I want to begin by intentionally moving away from discussing what we, as researchers, learned from the young participants in the focus groups, and instead spend time exploring what young people took away from participating in the conversations. Specifically, I want you to see how they understood, experienced, and articulated the benefit of these conversations to themselves.

In the preface to this book, I described storytelling as transformative, both for the storyteller and the listener. In the pages that follow, I hope you will see how the focus groups were more than research. They became meaningful conversations where participants shared and listened to personal stories, built trust, and supported each other's aspirations and dreams. In this way, the conversation acted as an intervention of sorts, creating a container in which participants had time and space to reflect on their own lives, consider their futures, and find validation in the shared experiences of others. Of course, as a moderator and researcher, I was not immune to the effects of storytelling and story listening. In the final pages of this chapter, I will briefly reflect on how the experience of listening to young people in this way changed how I approach research with young people and how I think about my own education, career, work, and life.

HOW THE STORY SERVES THE STORYTELLER

In chapters 2 and 3, I wrote about some of the similarities and differences among the young men who participated in the New York focus group, which was comprised of young people with a diversity of life and learning experiences. While some arrived at the group with clearly articulated aspirations and roadmaps for their future lives and careers, others had spent little or no time considering how their lives after high school might look or feel. Some participants had already discovered something they were passionate about pursuing and others had not. Some had been exposed to and committed themselves to traditional education and career pathways, while others were trying to figure out how to plan for their careers in other ways. Some had parents, guardians, teachers, and other adults with whom they spoke about their interests and who helped them cultivate a sense of their talents and abilities, where they felt they belonged, and how they would reach their goals. Others did not have this support. In short, the focus groups in New York and elsewhere featured a high degree of heterogeneity and included participants with vastly different expectations of and preparations for the world beyond high school. Far from derailing the conversation, these differences helped to support an experience in which almost everyone in the group had an opportunity to be a resource or offer words of encouragement or support at one moment or another: everyone got to be an expert. As if mountain climbers, students were able to *lift* each other from a range of different vantage points and perspectives.

THE POWER OF A *LIFT*

In New York, the dynamic between Lyrik and some of the other young men in the group illustrates this phenomenon of *lifting*. You may recall from the previous chapters that Lyrik was a senior in high school and entered the focus group, seemingly resigned to low expectations for himself and his life. Lamar and

Cedric had already made strides toward careers as an actor and an HVAC technician, respectively. Xavier and Lukas were living with their chosen families, having built non-familial relationships that supported them and their aspirations.

Early in the discussion, Lyrik expressed uncertainty about his future and a great deal of self-doubt about his own abilities. He described himself as overly negative and worried about struggling financially as an adult. Here Lyrik responds to the provocation to imagine his life at age twenty-five.

LYRIK: *For me, twenty-five would look like probably living in a crappy apartment somewhere in the five boroughs.*
LUKAS: *Dude, let's not say that.*
LAMAR: *. . . don't do that. Shoot for the stars.*
XAVIER: *Move in with me.*
LYRIK: *I'll have roommates. One of them is probably going to be a little smelly.*
LUKAS: *You said five?*
MALCOLM: *Why he got to be smelly? Why can't he just be a regular . . .*
LYRIK: *I'm living in the five boroughs. I'm going to need some roommates. Rent is expensive.*
MALCOLM: *Oh, my God. I need you to think bigger than this, than living in some crappy apartment.*
XAVIER: *Instead of a five-bedroom apartment, he's got a five-bedroom house.*

When Lyrik describes his expectations for his life at age twenty-five, Lamar, Xavier, Malcolm, and Lukas respond with *lifts*, telling him that he can and should aim higher. This dynamic continues throughout the remainder of the conversation, where Lyrik is often the recipient of *lifts* and Malcolm, in particular the provider of them. In other parts of the discussion, it is Malcolm who tells Xavier that his dream of gaming is possible, and applauds Cedric, as we heard in chapter 3, for having the wherewithal to get training as an HVAC technician.

CEDRIC: *I go to a program and I do HVAC there. I was doing that since last year. It's my second year, so I get my certification this year.*
MALCOLM: *Congratulations brother. Nice, that's lit.*
LAMAR: *That's what's up.*
MALCOLM: *They need more Black people like you out there in the world.*
CEDRIC: *Thank you.*

In reflecting on this notion of *lifting*, I found myself drawn back to Malcolm's pathway with renewed curiosity. During the introductions, Malcolm said he was twenty-one and working in fashion as a stylist and shopper at a retail store. When he shared his pathway with the group, he started out by saying that he had made some bad decisions and then went on to talk about his goals of finding love, "someone to respect," getting married, and starting a family. In the pathway image and also in the conversation, he alluded to some of the emotional growth he would need to do to bring these things into fruition, including "finding better (self) worth" and overcoming "inner demons." Malcolm, although working at a career that he seemed to like and identify with, seemed to frame his career choice as more of an enabling condition for the life that he wanted to lead, not the purpose of life itself. In describing his interests and goals he said, "I try not to limit myself to one thing because I know I would just be as happy in doing any of those."

MALCOLM: *I mean . . . starting from now, so a retail job, bad choices. Meaning bad choices that got to the job I got now that's pretty much what that means. Finding a better job, and then, you know, after that, love comes in, after that, finding a career, then married, kids, making a statement, own business, and then retire.*

You know, it's so funny. Career is a different word for me than most people because I do so many things. Yes, styling is the main thing I do, but, you know, I do like this little YouTube thing with my boy. So like I feel like God blessed me with so many different talents that something is going to lead to the career that I want. Like I have to say . . . I was really blessed to be smart and just take it all in. I try not to limit myself to one thing because I know I would just be as happy in doing any of those. You know what I mean?

As we saw on page 74, he goes on to describe his imagined future at age forty-five, when he imagines many of his personal and career goals will have been realized.

MALCOLM: *You know, two kids, maybe three living it up, happy, family. I got my own place. I mean, I got my own business. I got my own, boo, yeah, my guy. I really work as much as I want, so I guess I can say if I want to work 9:00 to 5:00, I work 9:00 to 5:00, so I can be home for the kids afterwards. If I want to work later at night, so I can be home throughout the day to take them to school, you know, it just depends on how I feel. So I can say anywhere between 35 to 40 hour, you*

CONVERSATION AS INTERVENTION   81

FIGURE 4.1   Malcolm's Pathway Image

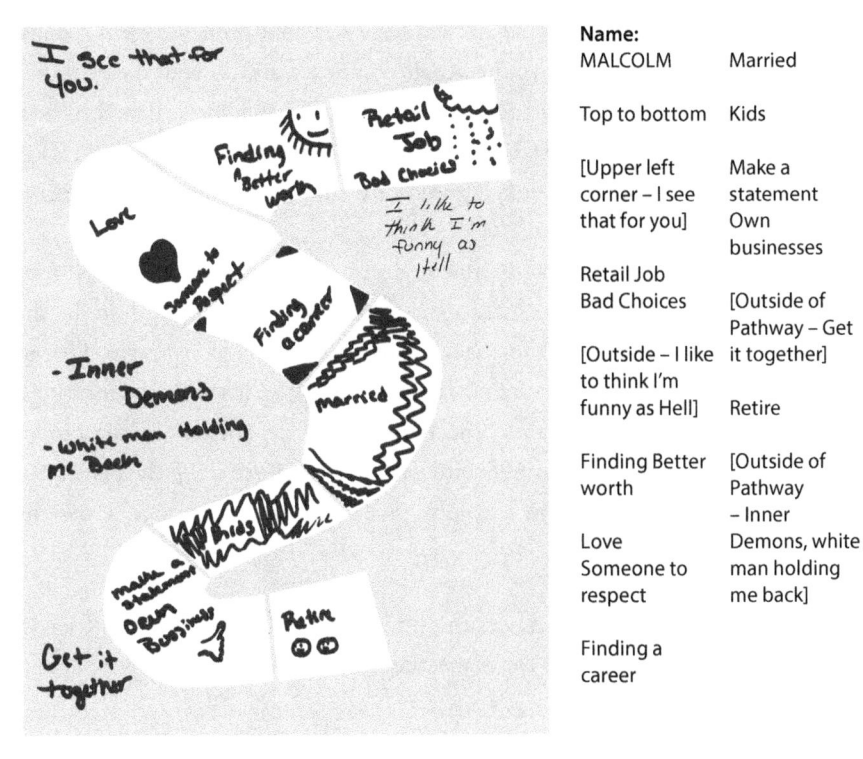

Name:	
MALCOLM	Married
Top to bottom	Kids
[Upper left corner – I see that for you]	Make a statement Own businesses
Retail Job Bad Choices	[Outside of Pathway – Get it together]
[Outside – I like to think I'm funny as Hell]	Retire
Finding Better worth	[Outside of Pathway – Inner Demons, white man holding me back]
Love Someone to respect	
Finding a career	

know, just a regular hours, but just obviously, because I'm the boss, I can make or break those hours if I want to.

But I really do genuinely want to give back to my family, my mother, especially my mom. Like she is one of the main reasons I go as hard as I do because of my mom . . . I want to work for people who I know got me to the point where I'm at right now.

We don't know how much of what he says about his own potential is objectively true; we only know that this is how he saw himself or wanted to be seen on that day. As I read through Malcolm's words and remember him in the room, I am struck by the themes around love and family in Malcolm's path and how this relates to the ways in which he *lifts* the other young men in the group. At age twenty-one, only a few years older than the youngest person in the group, Malcolm took on an almost familial role—something akin to an older cousin. I wonder now if Malcolm's contributions to the group—where he so clearly cared for and tended to the dreams of others—were an extension of the role he wanted to play in his own life.

WALKING AWAY WITH MORE THAN JUST A CHECK

In addition to the support participants gave one another during the focus groups, the conversation also provided young people with space to talk about their dreams, reveal their insecurities and find out, to the surprise of some, that others their own age were also in the mess of *striving*; trying to figure out what medium- and long-term goals to pursue and identifying the steps they would need to take to get them to their imagined futures.

At the end of each focus group, the moderator would ask participants if they had any final thoughts they wanted to share and how they might describe the conversation they'd had with someone outside of the room; for example, a friend they might talk to later that evening. In many instances, it was in the meetings' final moments that participants reflected on their experiences in the group, and provided us with some insights into what they believed to be the benefits of the conversations. Here is how the young men in New York talked about the experience.

MODERATOR: When you think about this discussion, and you talk to your friends, or to your family, whoever you're meeting with, what are you going to say this conversation was about?

CEDRIC: *It was about life.*

LAMAR: *Reminding myself that there are people like me. People that got big goals, big dreams. People that got the mindset I've got. You know, we all going to make it. It's not just we're all stuck in the rat race.*

ALI: *I think that like now I'm kind of like thinking like when I see somebody in the street, like we're all similar, but at the same time, we're all different. Like I just noticed, we all have like a lot of similarities just in terms of our mindsets. But at the same time, like we have different lives, obviously. We have different circumstances, situations. More of us should be talking to more people. Because, like, I grew from this conversation alone.*

XAVIER: *That's what's up.*

ALI: *So like just talking to more people would be better, I guess.*

LUKAS: *Just everybody's different perspective, it gave me a lot of insight. And I was exposed to a lot of different like a lot of ways that other people think. It was like a good reminder that, you know, we're all different, but we're really all the same.*

MILES: *Yeah, you think about it. Even though we're all different. We all have . . . something negative and positive going on in our life. And we're all have something that we're just trying to reach at the end of the day.*

XAVIER: *Even if you don't know what it is now . . .*

LAMAR: *Deep down there's . . .*

XAVIER: *. . . you have an aspiration. You just don't know what it is yet.*

CEDRIC: *We all got to get into what we want to do, we just got to get there first.*

XAVIER: *Because like . . . as kids, we went through like one hundred different aspirations in a week. Now is the time for all of us to fully decide what the aspiration is going to be.*

As they exited the focus group room, young people expressed gratitude for the opportunity to participate in the conversation and learn from their peers. Sometimes a participant would ask me about the moderator job, wondering why they'd never heard of people who conducted research for a living and wanting to know where or how they could learn more. Time and again, young people who were strangers to one another at the beginning of the two-hour discussion would exchange Instagram handles with other focus group participants on their way out, saying that they planned to keep in touch or, like Lamar in the previous chapter, they would ask to take home the pathway image that they'd filled out—saying that it would remind them of the gaps they need to fill in, and also where they want to be in the future.

The value of research is often determined by whether or not the findings generated novel findings in the aggregate. But I hope you can see how this research found value at the individual level as well. It wasn't just the outcomes of the conversation—the words spoken or the interpretations we, as adult researchers, made—but also the meaning that both the group and individual young people gave to their own conversations. In this context, being heard—both listening and speaking—felt deeply important.

During the conversations, they saw and heard from other young people who were grappling with similar questions about their lives and trajectories, which in turn validated their struggles to grow up, make plans, and work toward these plans. They were able to provide guidance, advice, and support for the others in the room—and we could see how much those lifts buoyed their self-confidence and stoked their motivation to pursue the futures they envisioned for themselves.

They reflected on the activities, like the pathway image, as if they were new tools that they could possibly use to figure out where they wanted to go in their lives, and the steps they could take to get there.

In other words, many of the young people in our focus groups experienced the conversations as an intervention, and per Ali's comment above, participating in conversation was an intervention worth seeking out. While the scope of this particular intervention might not have led directly to lasting effects—without longitudinal research, there's no way of knowing—I feel that the intervention effect I observed was powerful enough to merit sharing some of the design elements in this book, to encourage those of you reading to facilitate and support the creation of spaces where young people feel free to talk about their hopes, dreams, and futures in nonjudgmental and generative settings. There is so much opportunity to adapt and experiment with these conversation structures to build more spaces where young people feel they can express themselves and learn from—and be inspired by—their peers.

A CONVERSATION BY DESIGN

Telling one's story in the context of a focus group requires vulnerability. Think about the stories and quotes you've read in the previous three chapters. Perhaps, by now, you can hear whispers of their voices in your own head, recounting their stories and sharing their experiences. Maybe you can hear Lukas telling the group that he had to leave home and was in the process of making himself better. Or Xavier, who was building a chosen family after leaving his own family as a young teenager. Or Malcolm talking about his experience of being gay and Black and reflecting on how he opens with a laugh to set others, and perhaps himself, at ease. Or, perhaps, it's Lyrik's voice, worrying that his dreams are too small.

Whatever voices you recall, I hope you can see and appreciate that young people in these focus groups got personal—about themselves and with each other. How, in the course of a two-hour conversation, did the group establish this level of trust and camaraderie? How is it that these eight young men who entered the room as strangers left promising to keep one another accountable? Keeping Cedric on task for his HVAC certificate and business, keeping Lamar feeling positive about his auditions and his pathway to becoming an actor, and Xavier seeing that his dream of managing his own online team is within reach?

Before launching the *Striving to Thriving* project, my team and I talked to young people, peer researchers, youth development experts, educators, and others working on improving education and career pathways for youth. We learned that many young people, in and out of school, don't get opportunities to discuss their hopes and desires for their future lives. Through the design choices we made for *Striving to Thriving*, we wanted to ensure we were building a structure that would give young people ample opportunity and time to talk, plan, and, perhaps most importantly, imagine. Early in the research, we heard from participants how different the conversation in the focus group felt when compared to others in which they had participated. As a researcher, I feel it is important to better articulate what young people found special about *these* particular conversations.

ELEVATING STUDENTS' VOICES ABOVE THOSE OF ADULTS'

Across many settings and cultures, the role of the adult is almost always privileged above that of young people. Education, private and public organizations, government, and virtually all of the systems that touch young people's lives are centered on adult voices. To be clear, experiences and skills acquired over time matter, and children and young adults are moving through developmental stages so rapidly and in such different ways that adults correctly assume that their perspectives and viewpoints may be more ephemeral and prone to shift than our own. But this privileging of the adult perspective and authority means that spaces where young people are truly seen and allowed to speak must be created with more intentionality and thoughtful restraint.

The structure of the *Striving to Thriving* focus groups intentionally elevated and centered youth voices above that of the adult moderator in the room. These structured conversations offered young people an opportunity to imagine their future and think concretely about what their next steps could be. It was also a chance to talk and think big in a low-risk setting, absent the judgment and stress they sometimes feel when discussing their plans for their lives beyond high school. In those focus groups, the moderators posited themselves as neutral adults to help facilitate conversation among a group of youth participants. The adult moderators explained the context of the conversation and their role and that of the participants. The moderators needed to get through a series of questions they'd been given, and the participants were invited to share their honest opinions. The group was responsible for ensuring that the moderators could hear the "same amount from everyone in the group." Then the moderators went on to say they were hired to learn more about an issue or idea, but that they were not experts, and for this reason, all answers are right answers; in other words, the expertise lay with the young person or young people in the group and not with the adult.

All efforts were made to let the young people know that this conversation was about them and for them. And I think the moderator's comments throughout the two-hour session let the participants know in other ways that we, the adults, were fallible. We told them that it was possible that we might not understand everything they said and that we might need to ask them to clarify something or tell us more about what they meant *because they knew more about their lives and their experiences than we did*. We gave them permission to ask each other questions, too, normalizing the option that they might direct their questions about anything raised in the group to one another and *not to the sole adult in the room*. They asked and answered one another's questions, seeking advice, expertise, and validation from the others in the group and not from the adult.[2]

Since that time, I've worked on several other projects with young people at the center and I've come to believe that the setup and ground rules are everything. In the case of these particular focus groups, it was enough to do the type of table-setting we did at the beginning of the conversation. In other settings, when the ratio of young people to adults changes, young people need more advance preparation to understand what they are being asked to do. I've also learned from subsequent projects that age makes a difference—many middle schoolers do not warm up to the conversation as easily as those already fifteen to twenty-one years old. However, the level of intentionality remains a common thread; the purpose of research efforts like this is to get young people talking to each other as much or more than they do to the adults in the room because, in that way, the conversation creates the most benefit for *them*.

DIFFERENCE AS A POINT OF CONNECTION AND OPPORTUNITY

Earlier in this chapter, I noted the heterogeneity of the focus groups and how the differences in young people's goals and preparation to reach those goals contributed to instead of impeded the feeling of belonging within the groups. To explain why these differences matter, it is important to first understand how unusual it can be for young people who see themselves as different from one another to engage in conversation at this depth.

Consider for a moment the many ways that we segregate young people based on their goals, aspirations and interests. Sometimes it starts in school, where in an effort to close persistent achievement gaps, like those between Black and Hispanic students and their white counterparts, we often use criteria that drive young people into groups with greater and greater degrees of homogeneity. Think about it. Most Black and Hispanic students in the United States attend racially and economically segregated schools.[3] In this context, students who are perceived as academically motivated or talented are siphoned off as quickly and as efficiently as possible from students who are perceived as low achieving or under- or unmotivated. By high school, students have a sense of where they "belong" on the achievement continuum.

At a certain age, even some extracurricular programs and clubs focus almost exclusively on achievement, introducing or reinforcing narratives about what hard work and success look and feel like. When I'm being optimistic I can see that sometimes this segregation by academic achievement, motivation, or area of interest, can be positive or at least neutral. Sometimes it helps students to get the education that they deserve. Those who are bored can learn at an accelerated pace, and those who feel lost can receive the additional help and support they need. And sometimes this segregation is organic, with young people choosing to spend time in groups of peers who are similar to themselves in some way. Adolescents may want to spend time, for example, with peers with whom they share interests.

I share this context because the logic that informed our recruitment process and our focus group discussions—that young people with vastly different levels of confidence and clarity around their future goals can actually help one another—seems to be in stark contrast to the way that a lot of support for young people is designed. We have a proliferation of extracurricular programs that intentionally group students not only by their race or gender or both—but also by their perceived ability or academic motivation. And these efforts to ensure students get what they need—often students who for too long have been completely overlooked—inadvertently result in more and more homogenous groups and less and less contact with young people who are different from themselves. Programs that focus on career development and exploration and those that are more explicitly oriented toward pathways, where students choose something specific to pursue as a future career, are, by definition, in the business of segmenting students by interest. But I feel that our research and the conversations you've read in this book indicate that we, as a field, should proceed with caution. When our criteria places too much weight on whether young people know what they want to do for work, we may be unintentionally replicating a tracking system that many of us reject, thereby narrowing the peer supports that young people, especially Black and Hispanic young people, can find around them and in their own communities and classrooms.

Because of these drivers toward homogeneity or this refusal to recognize the diversity of experiences within groups, in particular within racial groups, young people risk limiting the peers with whom they engage. Notably, this narrowing of the groups with whom young people interact and learn persists even as educators and researchers are increasingly noticing the importance of broadening and deepening peer and social networks in service of building stronger and more supportive relationships. In other words, some of how we are designing for young people, may be limiting their ability to learn from and engage with peers who are different from themselves.

Over and over again, young people in this research project expressed their appreciation for the opportunity to hear the diversity of experiences informing the attitudes and outlook their peers shared about their future lives. Their different lived experiences, pathways, and visions for their futures added to, rather than undermined, the sense of belonging that emerged in the groups. Participants appreciated that each came to the table with different challenges, and questions, and they celebrated the ability to share ideas, *collectively* figure things out and see themselves, and act as resources for one another.

There is something powerful about watching young people with different life experiences, perspectives, and opinions gather in a room and care for one another's dreams. In the pages you've just read, I wrote that the young people who participated in these conversations were changed by the experience. I would be remiss to say that that is where the transformation ended. Being in conversation with strangers changes us. Perhaps it comes from the opportunity to be both teacher and learner, to share our own experiences, and to, at times, have those experiences be validated by others—or drawn out—or built upon. Or just left alone, given a beat—seen for just the right amount of time. Perhaps it is in those moments that we find the greatest value. Being in conversation changes us all, including the adults in the room. After all, we are social, storytelling animals in this way. Our minds are changed and sharpened in collaboration with those around us. But I will tell you that as we listened to young people in conversation, the adults in the room were also changed. This experience changed me too.

LISTENING AS AN INTERVENTION

On a personal level, this project was a revelation. I cannot overstate how devastated I felt in the years when these focus groups were taking place and when I was in my earliest years as a parent. My son was born in 2016, two days before Donald Trump won that year's Presidential election. What followed often felt like a near-daily lynching of Black and Brown boys by the police, one that showed the continual and unabated rise of the most blatant white supremacy I had seen in my lifetime. Every education project I worked on reminded me that my son's light could be snuffed out instantly. If not physically by the police, then emotionally by an education system that was designed to fail him and others who look like him.

Given this, it felt profound to sit among Black young people, in particular boys and young men, as they spoke with one another, grappling with what it meant to be young, to be moving toward adulthood, and to be actively imagining and working toward the futures they envisioned for themselves. I felt that I was doing something that mattered. I was helping to build spaces where boys and men could talk about their aspirations, fears, goals, and dreams—things the greater society often politicized but rarely interrogated.[4]

My work on *Striving to Thriving* also led me to reflect on my professional choices: my decision to build a career solving problems through narrative and messaging. The research has forced me to confront certain realities about the work that I do, and for whom, and how the choices we make as researchers sometimes introduce or perpetuate harmful narratives about Blackness and youth and the intersections between the two.

But perhaps the place where I see the greatest change in myself is how I think about and understand my own narrative about education, career, and work, the patterns of stories I tell about my own experience, and how I decided to do the work that I do. I interrogated the ways in which I benefitted from education and workforce systems that value a specific set of milestones and accomplishments, such as high GPAs and performance on standardized tests. A system that values and mythologizes my story: that of a Black child of a single Black mother who got good grades, stayed out of trouble, graduated high school early, and proceeded to college. I look more carefully at the broader cultural narratives to which I was exposed, which promised a family-sustaining income to those who never questioned the path laid out for us. A path, that for me, was reinforced by teachers, counselors, and my parents. I was told that the path would pay off, if only I stayed the course. I, saturated in messaging that told me to succeed and also told me what success would look like when I got there, reached out and grabbed the rings in front of me—swinging from one to the next. I experienced my education as a roadmap—and I was proud when I reached my destination—a collection of college degrees and jobs that paid the rent in cities of my choosing.

Like me, you have your own experiences with some of the systems that make up the pathway from K–12 education to career and work. If you are honest with yourself, you might find that, like me, you may have a stake in making sure this blatantly unequal system—one that validates and values our own success stories, our own choices, and indeed many of our own career pathways—remains intact.

Even as we advocate for more resources, we allocate those resources to structures that seem fundamentally designed to fail a majority of students. We champion career-connected learning, STEM education, new technologies, and emergent pathways but stop miles short of committing ourselves to the radical reimagining of our education and workforce systems that this moment demands. This type of transformative change will require us to create new narratives about young people who are Black and Hispanic and those who are poor, and new narratives about ourselves as changemakers.

All of these reflections bring me back to stories and listening. Yes, there are decades of statistics that show that the barriers facing Black and Brown young people still persist. But I believe that by listening to young people, and following their lead, we can keep moving forward with hope.

CHAPTER 5

Guidance, Frameworks, and Parting Thoughts

It would go against the purpose of this book to simply share stories and observations and leave it at that. Many of us working to change education and early career experiences for young people do so because we are committed to a more equitable and just future. Our field is diverse, and each of you will find different ways to apply the insights and thinking presented here. I have written this final chapter to assist you in making connections between the book and your practice. I will share suggestions for how to center young people's voices in the translation and dissemination of research about them, translate key insights from the research into narrative and messaging recommendations for those communicating with and about young people, and highlight frameworks and ideas from earlier chapters that can be adapted or used to support program and policy design.

CENTERING YOUNG PEOPLE'S VOICES IN RESEARCH DISSEMINATION

In the years since completing *Striving to Thriving*, my team and I developed a series of reports, a website, and other communication assets, sharing what we learned and making the research insights feel more approachable and actionable. To develop these materials, we reviewed toolkits and research reports that encouraged adults to listen to young people. Our review included publications such as *With Learners, Not for Learners: A Toolkit for Elevating Learner Voice in CTE*, created by Advance CTE (Career and Technical Education), and YouthPrise and Every Hour Counts' *Powered by Youth Voice: Future Directions for Afterschool.*[1]

Using these and other examples as inspiration, my colleagues and I developed a visual brand and dissemination plan for *Striving to Thriving*. Early in our design and dissemination work, we knew we had to balance the needs of our adult audience with what we felt to be a moral obligation to foreground young people's words, images, and stories in the research materials. This commitment to centering young people's voices influenced the following decisions, and we

- held an open call for youth artists around the themes of the research and incorporated their photography and artwork into the design of the website for *Striving to Thriving* research. Equitable Futures, https://www.equitablefutures.org, is its primary dissemination platform and a clearinghouse for other reports and resources connected to the Gates Foundation's pathways strategy;[2]
- incorporated vivid colors, youthful imagery, geometric designs, and an artistic rendering of the pathway image into the *Striving to Thriving* brand, extending the metaphors young people used to describe their pathways and reinforcing the personal identities of young people's journeys;
- created a toolkit, also available on the Equitable Futures website, *Designing Pathways with Young People*.[3] The toolkit's components included an assessment tool that allowed users to measure and diagnose their progress on adopting youth voice, a searchable online quote library made up of hundreds of anonymized youth quotes from focus group transcripts, a set of Design Principles, and a series of worksheets (one is included later in this chapter and the appendixes), that gives guidance on adapting the pathways exercise to programmatic work.

Throughout 2020–2022, my colleagues and I used the website and the accompanying suite of tools and resources we had developed as the basis for in-person and online presentations for audiences nationwide. We engaged with policymakers, researchers, educators, counselors, and narrative change strategists, and heard a great deal of interest in and excitement about our project findings and approach. As we learned more about what resonated with audiences, we refined our presentations to meet their interests, and focused on specific findings or dimensions of the research. As I noted earlier in this book, after several months we began to feel increasingly and uncomfortably distant from the young people who had entrusted us with their stories. We altered our presentations again, but this time to bring audiences into closer proximity to young people's stories. For example, we started anchoring our discussions about the research with the pathway metaphor. We also intentionally coupled young people's quotes *and* pathway images as a way to more dynamically introduce research participants and their stories. We found that when we shared the pathways images—tangible research artifacts created by young people—our audiences *connected*—the handwriting, strikethroughs, spelling, and colors added richness and depth to audiences' experiences and immersed them more completely in young people's stories. They witnessed the diversity and individuality of the research participants—how young people saw and talked about themselves, their aspirations, the support they had or would need, and the challenges they thought they might encounter.

The efforts my colleagues and I made to center youth voices in *disseminating* the research inspired us to consider and change how we *conduct* research with young people. In subsequent projects, we have engaged young people earlier and more completely in every phase of our research process: in planning, design, implementation, analysis, and dissemination. We considered at each phase how we could best collaborate with young people and elevate their knowledge and expertise. Here are some examples of how this looks in practice.

- We have engaged young people as co-designers of our research, subject-matter advisors, and content creators who help us develop and test narrative strategies and messaging prototypes
- We partnered with a non-profit, BUILD Inc, and trained a panel of youth advisors to collect data and conduct analysis of qualitative research.[4]

NARRATIVE AND MESSAGING RECOMMENDATIONS

I began this book by pointing out that we are saturated in narratives that tell us to believe Black and Hispanic young people are in a perpetual state of crisis—that, measured in the aggregate, these groups of young people are "falling behind" on many accepted metrics of educational and career success, such as test scores, college admissions, and job placement and advancement. I noted that while structural and generational resource inequities are often part of the explanation for racial and ethnic disparities in educational achievement, dominant narratives often misattribute these disparities to individual successes and failures—the idea that some young people simply lack the confidence, life experience, motivation, and resilience to exercise agency in their own lives. These young people, often Black, Hispanic, and/or poor, are encouraged to make decisions about their lives swiftly, discouraged from career exploration, and reminded (emphatically) that while other students may have the luxury of "failing fast and often," students like themselves do not. The directive is clear: One's life pathway is linear, and one must navigate it without delay to successfully achieve life goals. Additionally, a career is inserted as the most urgent of goals to which one must aspire.

The stories and voices in this book suggest that the dominant narratives that frame Black and Hispanic young people's identities as deficits do not match how young people experience or think about themselves and their futures. While this research project was not designed to explore narrative explicitly, our insights about how young people see themselves have clear implications for how we communicate with and about Black and Hispanic young people, and how we talk about and treat their aspirations for their future lives. Even if you are not directly involved in communications or narrative change, each of us, as advocates, policymakers, funders, or educators, has a role to play. In those moments when we are trying to create a sense of urgency to mobilize our peers and other partners in our ecosystems to develop and resource the solutions and ideas that will advance educational and economic equity, we have an obligation to be intentional about the stories we tell and the narratives we reinforce. While dominant crisis narratives about Black, Hispanic, and/or poor young people can't be shifted overnight, I'm confident that by centering young people's voices and stories, such as those shared in this book, we can begin to counter some of the most distorted narratives that continue to impede progress.

So, what does that look like? Our research suggests the following strategies:

- **Use asset-based framing to describe young people and their experiences.** While some groups of young people face more systemic barriers to educational and career success than others, individual young people possess

unique and rich visions about their future lives, even though they may be at different stages of thinking through how to get there.[5]
- **Use and socialize language that young people use themselves.** Young people don't shy away from naming themselves, their identities, and their experiences. If we mean "Black youth," let's use that language and not euphemisms or coded language that can be misinterpreted. If we want to describe young people's racial and ethnic identities in terms that resonate and feel meaningful to them, we must ask them directly what language they use and prefer. We cannot rely solely on what is deemed correct (e.g., Hispanic, Latino, Latinx, Brown) or on trend.
- **Celebrate and acknowledge agency.** Young people value their ability to make choices for themselves and determine how their lives will unfold. Whether they experience this positively or negatively, they understand themselves to be the most important decision-makers around their future goals. As advocates, we need to tread lightly here. We must balance young people's developmental and emotional need to practice and express personal agency and to see the potential impacts of that agency with our awareness and attentiveness to the systemic barriers that may impede their progress. Here, too, we must examine the notion that "adults know best" and that purely because of our age and accomplishments, we are better positioned to make choices for the young people in our lives. We must continually question the role that we and our programs play in young people's lives and how that role helps them to direct and make choices for themselves. We must examine our role as providers of safe spaces where young people can practice decision-making skills in low-risk settings, building the confidence they need to make bigger and higher-stakes decisions.
- **Embed mutuality.** Young people want to see themselves as contributing to conversations with caring adults in their lives (mentors, employers, teachers, etc.). They believe that authentic relationships, including those with a caring adult, are not one-sided but instead should be beneficial to both the young person and the adult. For these relationships to feel real, young people need to understand why an adult cares. Our messaging and programming should not be vertical, implying that young people have nothing of value to offer, and are merely vessels for an adult's knowledge or compassion, but instead uplift and highlight how young people's presence in a relationship,

discussion, or program matters in some way. In "mattering," the relationship with an adult is unique to each young person. It is emergent and comprises both what the young person *and* the adult bring to the table.

- **Assign equal value to student and adult expertise.** Young people know that there is information, life experiences, or other sources of knowledge they either don't have access to or have not encountered yet. There is no need to remind them of this by privileging adult voices above their own. As we reach out to, recruit, and communicate with young people, we need to remind ourselves to balance the knowledge and expertise that we know comes with age and experience with the very real knowledge that young people hold about what it feels like to be young right now. It is a tension of opposites—while adults have some information that young people do not, the knowledge adults hold is no more valuable than that held by youth.

ACTIVATING RESEARCH INSIGHTS TO INFORM PRACTICE

For all of the interventions and services that exist for young people, particularly Black and Hispanic young people, very little research exists that captures how they see themselves and the pathway to their future work and careers—the essence of occupational identity formation.[6] At its core, *Striving to Thriving* was intended to address that dearth of knowledge, with the hope that the insights from this project would be relevant and actionable to policymakers, educators, curricula designers, communications strategists, and funders. However, research insights, while often fascinating, don't always spark immediate ideas for application or action. Therefore, I want to spend the remainder of the chapter discussing some of the insights and emergent frameworks from this research and sharing some thoughts on how both can be used to inform your practice. I will begin by recapping the two frameworks already introduced in this book and then introduce one more.

In chapter 1, I shared our framework *Surviving, Striving, and Thriving*. You can think of this as a meta-framework derived from what young people said about how they related to work and working. The framework was developed in partnership with a cognitive linguist, who worked alongside our team, helping us to surface underlying metaphors present within and across focus group discussions. In addition to *Surviving, Striving, and Thriving*, we developed two more analytical frameworks to analyze, make sense of, and organize the large amounts of data we collected. The frameworks helped us see, describe, and report on the complexity of young people's experiences. We wanted to be able to speak deeply about young people's emotions and lives so that our audiences would be less inclined to privilege one journey over another.

The first analytical framework, *Five Occupational Pathways*, introduced in chapter 3 and discussed in more detail in the following section, helped us to understand the differences between how young people shape and articulate goals and how they conceptualize and imagine the steps that will take them to reach their goals. The second analytical framework, *Exposure, Exploration, and Selection*, discussed toward the end of this chapter, helped us to explain the stages young people move in and out of as they form and refine their occupational identities.

These last two frameworks strike a necessary balance between young people's developmental and emotional need to express agency in their own lives, and the information, resources, and assistance that adults can and must provide in supporting young people to discover and pursue their interests and engage in decision-making. These frameworks also serve as a reminder that one essential part of providing young people with support is understanding what they have already been exposed to and have experienced in their day-to-day lives, and what they *wish* to experience as they navigate the path toward adulthood.

Before moving into a discussion of each framework, I want to acknowledge the inherent tension in promoting and advocating for the centrality of youth voices and the critical importance of individual experiences and stories, and then introducing frameworks—typically provided to make meaning at the aggregate level. These concepts conflict, and my request that you truly listen and respond to individual youth experiences may feel oppositional to the notion of frameworks, which often assign people, ideas, and concepts to overly rigid categories.

Given this tension, I am sharing these final frameworks in the same way I have presented the other findings from this research. I encourage you to treat the frameworks as tools, instead of instructions, that can support you in designing programs, initiatives, and other interventions that resonate with young people and meet them where they are.

Framework #1: Five occupational pathways

The *Five Occupational Pathways* framework was derived from the pathway activity described in chapter 1, which youth research participants completed during interviews and in-person focus groups. The exercise gave young people a hands-on and tangible way to engage in questions that could otherwise prove elusive or overly abstract, such as: Where do you want to be as an adult? Where do you see yourself now, and what steps, stages, opportunities, and experiences will you need to pass through to get from point A (where you are now) to point B (where you want to be)? In chapters 1 and 2, you saw examples of completed pathways in the context of stories of young people from Belle Glade, Greenville, Oakland, and New York.

As researchers, the pathways exercise gave us a bridge to understanding the dreams and aspirations young people hold for themselves and their lives. The images also provided insight into how they organized their thinking about their future life and career goals and perceived the journey ahead. As we reflected on how multiple groups of young people engaged with the pathways visual, we noticed that many characterized the quality of their lives at the end of their pathway using similar terms, such as ownership, financial independence, having a family, and being able to travel (i.e., *thriving*). Nevertheless, they described differences in how well-equipped they felt to set life and career goals and how confident they were that they possessed or could locate the information, resources, and people they would need to achieve their goals. These differences in confidence and how equipped young people felt about their plans toward their future goals can be described in five pathway archetypes, ranging from those who know what their goals are and the steps they need to get there to young people who are unsure of both their goals and next steps. Examples of pathway archetypes 1 and 2 can be found in chapter 3.

Five occupational pathways

Pathway 1: *Know* what they want to do and *know* how to get there

Pathway 2: *Not sure* what they want to do, yet they *have a good idea* of the steps to take to explore to get there

Pathway 3: *Know* what they want to do, but they are *unsure* how to get there

Pathway 4: *Not sure* what they want to do and *unsure* of what steps to take

Pathway 5: *Know* what they want to do and *think they know* how to get there, but their imagined pathway is inaccurate and/or unrealistic

Although we ended up with five archetypes of occupational pathways, I urge you not to think of these as static categories. Instead, I hope you focus on how you might use this framework, or something similar to it, as an opportunity to engage in more authentic conversations with young people and to assess how they are feeling about their future lives without imposing unreasonable expectations about where you think they *ought* to be. By appreciating where young people see themselves in their journeys toward adulthood and their future careers, we can better adapt our work to support them and create the opportunities and interventions they need. In other words, I hope you treat the five occupational pathways as a potential catalyst for your conversations about careers and work with young people and guidance for how you might make meaning and derive possible actions from those conversations.

A word of caution. It can be tempting to use the occupational pathways exercise prescriptively—a classification system for students. Don't. The occupational pathways exercise is not a way to assign young people to rigid categories. After all, these categories were created by adults. Think of it more as something you have in your back pocket.

In chapter 4, I shared how the conversations among peers functioned as an intervention for some participants. Among these young people the pathways exercise was particularly meaningful. Several participants asked to take the pathways worksheet—which they had used to map out their career and life goals, and the steps they felt they needed to take to get there—home with them, as a roadmap or a reminder of where they wanted to be.

The value young people saw in the exercise inspired us to reimagine the pathway activity as a tool for adults working directly with young people and their families. You can find the complete pathways exercise, translated into a possible activity for you to experiment with in your work, in appendix B of this book. If you are interested in engaging with the young people you support in similar ways, you can adapt this exercise to your context. For example, you might want to help young people forecast what their futures could look like; you may also want to use the exercise to understand whether the barriers that your program works to remove for young people are priorities for the young people themselves. Parents could complete the exercise to understand how confident their children are about their next steps, either near- or long-term, and whether the transitions between different educational and employment systems will require different types of support and resources.

In addition to the pathway exercise in the appendixes, we have also created some additional guidance to help you use the *Five Occupational Pathways* framework to reflect on your practice and get to know the young people with whom you work.[7]

Relate the categories to young people who you know
- Think about what you may already know about the pathways of the young people with whom you work.
- If you feel you know a group of young people well, you may be able to sort their pathways and their understanding of their goals and aspirations into each of the five pathway categories.
- If you know the group less well, you may choose to complete the "Mapping Life and Career Pathways with Young People" worksheet exercise with your group. If you do not work directly with young people, you might consider having a colleague or a trusted neutral adult conduct the pathways exercise. You can then review the worksheets young people complete and sort them into the five pathway categories.

Take a step back and see what you notice
- Are there more pathways clustered around one category? Are there themes that emerge in how young people think about and describe their goals and the steps to reach those goals?
- Are there gaps in information, support, or knowledge that young people have identified themselves or that you can identify?
- Are there barriers named by young people that your program can help to remove? What could your program do to better help young people overcome the challenges they anticipate they will encounter on their pathways?
- How does seeing young people's pathways categorized in this way connect to how your program supports or impacts young people's career goals and pathways?

Create some hypotheses for how you might redesign or tweak your program
- If you find your answers to the questions above reveal some new insights into your work, the next step might be to tweak or redesign your program strategy to better reflect how young people perceive and experience their career pathways and the opportunities you see to strengthen or expand your program's impact.
  - For example, if the pathways framework has helped you to understand that many young people you work with need help with setting goals

before they can articulate the specific steps to reach those goals, how might you change your program strategy to help young people explore different career goals and jobs?

Consider adding the pathways framework to your assessment practice
- Use the pathways framework as an assessment tool to understand the impact of your program or intervention on how young people think about their goals and aspirations.
- You might ask young people to fill out the pathways exercise when they enter your program or at the beginning of a school year and then again at the end of your program or the end of the school year and assess changes to their pathways over a specific period. For example, if you learn that the young people you work with primarily have occupational pathways in categories three, four, and five, you may want to assess how your program moves young people toward categories one and two.

Framework #2: Exposure, exploration, and selection

The second framework, and the one that is new to you—*Exposure, Exploration, and Selection*—concerns occupational identity development outcomes such as self-efficacy, agency, and belonging. Here, we explain how young people experience and want to experience the developmental stages that result in a cohesive occupational identity.

Much of the literature on identity formation centers on two concepts: first, the universal nature of experiencing and engaging with a series of conflicts throughout the human lifespan, and second, how resolving these internal and external experiences propels us to the next stage of growth.[8] Psychoanalyst Erik Erickson applied this theory specifically to adolescent development and argued that adolescent identity formation is made up of two parts: it begins with *crisis*, a time when one's values and choices, often related to our childhood selves, are being reevaluated, and is followed by *commitment*.[9] After a period of trying-on and experimentation we *commit* to various aspects of our identities including vocation, religion, relational choices and gender roles.[10]

The *Exposure, Exploration, and Selection* framework builds on these human development theories and applies them to young people's experiences of occupational identity development. In adolescence, young people begin to connect perceptions of the kind of life they want to live as adults, often gleaned from the adults that surround them, with the types of jobs, work, and careers that will enable or hinder them from obtaining that life. To understand what jobs, work, or careers might be a good fit for them, young people engage in an iterative assessment process, consciously or subconsciously, that can be understood as three distinct but interconnected stages: *exposure, exploration,* and *selection*. At each stage, young people make choices (conscious and subconscious) to accept, reject, or modify their progression in response to what they learn and experience.

Even writing a basic description of this framework, however, makes it sound more linear and tidier than it is. The framework of *Exposure, Exploration, and Selection* is meant to challenge us to consider how honest and realistic our depictions of occupational identity formation are. In order to determine which version of a "good life" and "good job" is right for them, young people need to experiment and explore during adolescence—a period during which they display openness and desire to engage in behaviors and appearances in search of their own unique identities. During this time, young people may cycle through a series of identities before finding the one that suits them best. This research shows that many young people expect to and want to engage in a similar process as they develop their occupational identities, that is, what they like to do, what they believe are their skills, and where they feel they belong. In other words, *exploration*—which often can feel unformed or indecisive to impatient adults—is especially valuable to young people as they begin to think more concretely about their futures.

In addition to referencing the literature on identity development, the framework also builds on the research of others working to define occupational identity formation. For example, before *Striving to Thriving* was underway, researchers Callahan et al. conducted a review of programs designed to facilitate occupational identity outcomes of self-concept, self-efficacy, and belonging, and developed a three-part framework for understanding influences and barriers tied to occupational identity outcomes: *Exposure, Engagement, and Participation*. While their framework drew upon program-level and evaluation data, ours relies directly on the insights and experiences of the young people we spoke with. We see these two frameworks as complementary.

In their review of influences on occupational identity in adolescence, Callahan et al. drew a distinction between *engagement* and *participation*. The authors described *engagement* as "including exposure but involving educational settings where young people are engaged in projects and acquiring skills" and *participation* as "including *exposure* and *engagement* [as] being part of and contributing to real-world professional life."[11] We found that young people in our research understood *engagement* and *participation* as overlapping (consistent with the Callahan framework), but that they collapsed or conflated these ideas into a larger social behavior focused on *exploration*. For example, many participants spoke about practice-based learning, internships, and high school pathways curricula as a process of trying out and exploring different ideas and career possibilities, and also a way of experimenting with identity more broadly.

Our framework includes *selection* to illustrate the decision-making young people engage in after they feel they have experienced *exposure* and *exploration*. In our research, we have seen that young people's selection of a career pathway can be iterative. As young people learn more about themselves and what they like and don't like to do, their selections become more refined and precise. Again, we see the two frameworks as complementary: Callahan et al. are focused on how programmatic interventions create occupational identity outcomes, and ours is focused on how young people experience this period of their development and relate to these stages with varying degrees of agency.

An iterative take on occupational identity development. Time may be linear, but the pathway to a career is not. The very notion of what counts as a career is in transition. What may have once felt like a binary decision upon graduating from high school—joining the workforce or attending a four-year college and thereby deferring joining the (full-time) workforce—has now, by almost all accounts, become more complicated.[12] This fact is not lost on young people. They are surrounded by adults who they have seen make diverse decisions about their own education and career pathways, such as enrolling in college and not completing it, not enrolling in college and attending other postsecondary training, working full-time after high school, returning to higher education after several years of work, a myriad of other circumstances, or some combination of any of the above.

Young people, like the young men in New York, had already seen their parents, siblings, cousins, and other family members celebrate and lament choices made, jobs taken or those missed out on, careers that met financial and emotional needs, and also those that didn't. In truth, many young people are already aware of the tensions, practical tradeoffs, and realities—the all-around complexity of building durable occupational pathways and how one builds the right path for themselves.

FIGURE 5.1

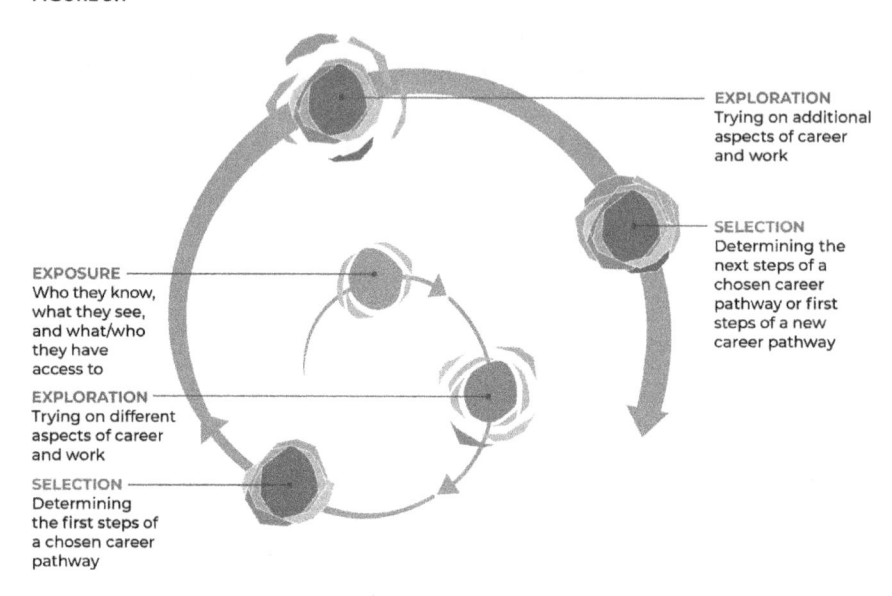

EXPLORATION
Trying on additional aspects of career and work

SELECTION
Determining the next steps of a chosen career pathway or first steps of a new career pathway

EXPOSURE
Who they know, what they see, and what/who they have access to

EXPLORATION
Trying on different aspects of career and work

SELECTION
Determining the first steps of a chosen career pathway

Given this messiness, it feels disingenuous to continue to frame youths' occupational identity development as linear, a one-shot deal. In the modern era of working, adults change careers several times, and this is projected to increase dramatically in the coming years.[13] People who are young now will become adults who must *explore* career options and try on career identities with greater frequency. We know that successful adults engage in an iterative process of assessing their strengths, skills, and interests at various moments in their lives, continually evaluating steps toward the "good life" and careers that best meet their needs. I would argue that when we learn more about ourselves, what we like and are good at doing, and what we don't like and struggle with, our decision-making improves; we are better informed and able to assess competing considerations.

How can we convey the inherent value of exploration and learning about oneself through meaningful work? Let's look at the framework more closely.

At the core of the *Exposure, Exploration, and Selection* framework are the ideas of youth agency and iterative identity development. As young people move through, in, and around these states, they learn more about the world of work and themselves. Equipped with this new information, they are able to refine their senses of what is desirable in a "good job" or career and better understand which careers match their own distinct "good job" qualities. They can then identify the steps, experiences, and knowledge they will need to work in a specific occupational field.

In the preceding chapters, you've read how young people value personal agency; they want to feel that they can exert control over their own lives, and they also want to see the effects of that agency—to feel some measure of self-efficacy. Our research participants were between the ages of 15 and 21, and many had not yet graduated from high school and were still considering the choices they would make in early adulthood. Because of their ages, they were better able to produce examples of *exposure* and *exploration* than of *selection*. However, in our discussions, we listened for and deeply considered their desires and predictions for how their careers and lives could unfold. We heard what they wanted—for the process to be forgiving and flexible and to be able to engage in behaviors and conversations that would help them figure out how and what they wanted their lives to be like. We also heard that they wanted to feel that they could continue to refine their ideas about the types of work they wanted to do, and adjust as time passed instead of feeling they may be locked into a career they didn't want without the skills to make new and better choices for themselves.

In each stage of our framework, young people experience increasing levels of agency. From *exposure*—which includes some of the more passive experiences of early childhood, when young people observe their parents and family members' behaviors, stories, and narratives of work, to *selection*, when young people use everything they know about themselves, the workforce, and their specific contexts, to determine what steps they will take to select and then initiate a path towards a career. The framework represents how young people want to experience occupational identity development: iterative and compounding, not fixed or static. It acknowledges that young people may return to the *exploration* and *selection* stages multiple times in their working lives, and perhaps more frequently in their first steps into the workforce when they may be more likely to transition across industries and types of work. For example, a young person may make an initial career pathway selection and then, in the process of working, gain exposure to other opportunities better suited to their skills and interests. This awareness of a new possibility may lead them back to an *exploration* stage before making a new and perhaps different selection.

Exposure is a time when children and then adolescents are absorbing (consciously and subconsciously) information about the world of work and the emotional and lived experience of working. In chapter 2, you read that some of the earliest influencers of young people's assumptions, expectations, and understanding of *jobs, work,* and *careers* are the adults present in their lives as they grow up. Parents, older siblings, cousins, and extended family provide intimate glimpses into working life. Young people's exposure to adults' stories and experiences of working informs what they imagine is possible or desirable for themselves. In other words, the *exposure* stage can be seen as a critical phase when young people draw boundaries around their imagined future selves—producing an early shape onto which they add greater detail as they grow and their world expands.

At the same time young people are piecing together the universe of *jobs, work,* and *career* possibilities to which they feel they *can* aspire, they are also learning more about themselves. They are learning what they like and dislike, their interests and strengths, and trying on, or experimenting with, different identities and ways of being. Through the adults in their lives, the media, and larger societal narratives around success, status, and belonging, they are learning the types of work, education, and achievements that hold value. Young people are also becoming knowledgeable about how education and family decisions impact career pathways and momentum. This includes learning about the impacts of decisions: whether to pursue postsecondary education, the timing of having children, and when to take on family obligations and debt. And these experiences can expand or constrain how young people perceive their futures—intentionally or unintentionally.

As young people are exposed to various jobs and careers, they continually assess what aspects of work and life match what they want for themselves and which do not. Assessment enables young people to do one, or a combination of, the following:

Accept: Young people see a job or career that they feel matches the life that they want for themselves and provides a minimum of the good job qualities they are seeking.[14]

Reject: Young people determine that they do not want the life that they see around them or determine that they do not want the jobs, work, or career that they see, know about, or have access to.

Modify: Young people determine that the jobs or careers they see have some of the qualities they want for themselves, and decide to modify what they see and explore other options.

Exploration occurs through exposure to occupations, engagement in occupational practices, and participation in occupational communities. In *exploration*, young people are seeking out experiences, information, and knowledge that will expand their universe of what jobs and careers exist and which might be a fit for them. Through *exploration*, young people develop images and associations about specific career pathways, acquire skills and knowledge relevant to specific careers and work, and sometimes develop relationships with adults who can support or assist them through these stages of their career and life journeys.

Recall that young people don't necessarily distinguish between *exploration* and *experimentation*. Instead, they focus on the experience of "trying on" their future selves and how this allows them to become surer of where they want to go next and who they want to be. Where elements of the *exposure* stage can feel passive, *exploration* is active. Young people want to select or seek out information and experiences that either reflect or expand their existing interests and skills. They do this or want to do this in a variety of settings.

- **Online:** Joining online occupational communities that allow meaningful participation from members with varying levels of skill in order to learn more about a job or career; such as engaging with social media accounts of individuals, organizations, or events connected to a type of work, work experience, identity, lifestyle, or geography
- **Entertainment:** Intentionally selecting media content (television, film, commercials, etc.) that shares information about jobs or careers through character-driven stories
- **Institutional:** Participating in programs, schools, or other institutions that provide young people with opportunities to experiment with different technical and occupational skills
- **Work:** Part-time or summer employment that gives young people an opportunity to earn money while learning more about a specific job or career in a real-world setting

Selection occurs when young people have more information about themselves, more knowledge about a specific job or career, and a growing sense of the life they want to lead. This new information helps them to determine the career goals they want to work toward and also helps them to identify the initial steps toward those goals. These initial steps can be as varied as young people themselves.

- Some young people choose to pursue a postsecondary education, including a two-year college, four-year college, vocational or technical education, or a certificate.
- Some connect with mentors, coaches, or other adults who can facilitate additional exposure or access to a specific educational/career pathway or a community of practitioners.
- Some are determined to break away from friends that they see as a distraction or impediment to the life course they want to pursue.
- Some will decide to make new friends, join clubs, or otherwise change and expand their social circles.

An argument for telling young people the truth. Too often, young people are made to feel as if every decision that lies ahead of them, or those they are making in real-time, have consequences that extend far into the future. They perceive that their choices are terminal in a sense—that they must make a singular life-defining decision about their future careers, and if something doesn't work out, or if they don't like it, they will have forfeited the opportunity to make another decision. In other words, they have heard too much about the *selection* part of the framework and not nearly enough about the *exposure* and *exploration* parts. This overemphasis on *selection* is especially true for young people who are on their own, or whose families do not have the wealth or the privilege to pay and allow for periods of *exploration*.

Right now, many career development programs, particularly those that target Black and Hispanic young people and young people from lower-income families, reinforce the perception that occupational identity moves in only one direction—terminating with the attainment of a high-quality or in-demand career. The terminal framing of a career is because we, as adult experts, feel the stakes are too high for young people who face systemic barriers to success to *explore* for too long.

To be clear, I am not proposing that we disregard or minimize the importance of figuring out how to earn a living wage. In our society, this plays an outsized role in the trajectory of one's life and comfort. Nor do I want to ignore the economic and geographic contexts that can sometimes constrain young people's choices and over which they have no control. Some young people are fleeing what they perceive to be a dearth of work opportunities in a specific location; others are confident they want to stay in the region where they grew up. Some young people cannot incur debt by attending college, and others have reservations about the value of a college degree. We cannot and should not overlook these factors. Instead, I am asking us to tell young people the truth.

I encourage you to reflect on your own occupational identity and career pathway. Notice the choices and inflection points that have changed how you thought about the career that best fits your personal version of a "good life." In what ways has your own occupational identity been iterative? How can you more explicitly share this truth: that even as adults, we are constantly making decisions to improve our career and work lives and that returning to phases of *exploration* and *selection* is not only expected but also valuable?

We could tell young people that one outcome of engaging in work and career is that we can see more choices for ourselves and more opportunities to continually refine our ideas about what constitutes a good job for *each* of us. And that as they gain more work and life experience, we give young people permission to return to that period of *exploration* where they will once again grapple with what job or career will most enable them to live a good life. Perhaps we could change what we measure—and introduce tools that allow us to assess young people's capacity to assess what is right for them, to make plans, and to exert agency as they pursue their goals and dreams. Perhaps we would tell young people that they are architects of the lives they wish to lead, not merely pawns progressing along a pathway that has already been established.

CONCLUSION

My intention with this chapter has been to give you something to take with you: concrete examples of how you might implement some of what we learned. It is always a struggle to strike the right balance between actionable insights that motivate readers to apply research findings and prescriptive recommendations. On the one hand, I want to extrapolate rich and meaningful insights that readers feel help them think differently about their work. At the same time, I want to ensure that the insights are not overly directive or prescriptive, telling the reader what to do and say. I hope that what I have shared in this and the previous chapters is helpful to you and that you have what you need to take action.

I will leave you with these final thoughts.

Trapping young people in crisis narratives not of their own making, and overlooking their agency and individual lived experiences, is not unique to the fields of education and career development. Adults in other fields fall into the trap of ignoring youth voices and agency, too. Yet youth also have a say in our collective future as a society. Youth-led movements around political elections, the environment, racial justice, and gender equality are all good indicators that older adults are not the only decision-makers in the room.

We share an obligation to tell new and different stories about and to young people, especially young people who are Black and Hispanic and those who come from lower-income communities.

In reading this book, I hope that you have encountered young people's voices and wisdom in new and different ways. For me, young people are a never-ending source of inspiration and hope. They show remarkable agency, resilience, and determination to succeed. That any of them don't is much more on us than on them.

Acknowledgments

To the young people who participated in this research:

I am humbled to have had the opportunity to sit with and among you as you talked, dreamt, and invented your future lives. I am grateful to have been entrusted with your stories, ideas, and imagined futures. I hope I've done you proud.

Despite coming from a family of writers, I profoundly underestimated the work of writing a book. Thank you to my family and friends for all the ways you have helped me carve out enough time to write, for your love, and your high tolerance for all the risks that I take. Thanks to the kiddo for sharing your joy, creativity, and imagination with me and your Dad. To my editors at Harvard Education Press, Jayne Fargnoli, and Karen Adler, I am grateful for your patience and your kindness. To my brilliant colleagues, Dr. Golnaz Arasatpoor-Irgens, Minna Jung, Robert Pérez, and Amy Simon—thank you for all the ways you make me smarter. Thanks to the generous support of the Bill & Melinda Gates Foundation, I had time to think and write. Tom, Carvell, and Maya, thanks for being brave and doing many of the hardest parts of life first (including writing books).

Finally, thank you Nancy Hoffman, Senior Advisor at Jobs for the Future. In 2021, Nancy and Emily Lockwood suggested I write a book about the Striving to Thriving research. I said yes, and here we are. Thanks to you both for believing that I had something important to say.

Onward.

APPENDIX A

Methodology

Because the conversations from the *Striving to Thriving* focus groups were so powerful, I gave them top billing in this book. However, other researchers working in this space will always be interested in the details of the methodology employed for this project. These details are available in the full-length report, *Striving to Thriving*, which is available, along with other research materials and resources, on the Equitable Futures website.

I co-led the *Striving to Thriving* research with Amy Simon, Founder and Principal of Goodwin Simon Strategic Research (GSSR), a public opinion research firm based in Oakland, California. What follows is the full methodology for the *Striving to Thriving* project written by GSSR and previously published in the *Striving to Thriving* report available on the project website.

RECRUITING AND SCREENING PROCESS FOR RESEARCH PARTICIPANTS

Goodwin Simon Strategic Research (GSSR) works with specialized recruiters in each location for the focus groups and in-depth interviews to contact, screen, and recruit potential research participants. These local recruiters rely on their existing participant database to reach potential participants. In some instances, they would also use a list of registered voters in the area that we provide. Recruiters also work with schools and local community-based organizations to reach potential recruits, post ads on social media, and distribute flyers at schools, shopping malls, or community centers. Potential recruits are offered a financial incentive if they qualify and attend. Once recruits arrive at the focus group facility (or hotel in locations where no facility exists), they are rescreened to ensure they qualify for the groups. We over-recruit to ensure that a sufficient number of participants show up and are qualified to participate. Any recruits who are dismissed after rescreening receive the same financial incentive as participants who are seated.

For the online survey, potential respondents are invited to participate from several panels of respondents maintained by an online survey vendor. While these panels typically comprise a diverse cross-section of respondents, they are somewhat less statistically representative of the nation's population than properly designed and conducted telephone surveys. Online users tend to be slightly younger, less rural, more educated and have higher incomes than the US population as a whole. However, these population differences are decreasing over time as more and more people in the United States are now online. Online surveys also fit people's increasingly digital lifestyles, especially now that the surveys can be designed to allow respondents to complete them on mobile devices. For young people, in particular, online surveys can be an excellent methodology, as the overwhelming majority of young people are online. In addition, there is some research showing that young people may be more honest in their responses to surveys when they are answering an online survey compared to when they are asked to reply to questions by an interviewer in person or via phone.

To participate in the survey, in-depth interviews, or focus groups, parents or guardians of research participants under age eighteen are required to provide their consent for their minor children. In each case, these parents or guardians are provided with a financial incentive—in addition to the financial incentive provided to their children. For the in-depth interviews and focus groups, parents and guardians are required to accompany minors to the facility and sign a consent form in person.

RESEARCH METHODS EMPLOYED

Individual in-depth interviews

Seven in-depth interviews were conducted with young people ages fifteen to twenty in November 2018. Three interviews were conducted in Gary, Indiana (two with Black females and one with a Black male), and four were conducted in Albuquerque, New Mexico (one with a Hispanic female, two with Hispanic males, and one with a white male). These interviews allowed us to develop a more in-depth understanding of how young people think and talk about their identity formation, how they relate it to their education and work goals, and the challenges they face in achieving those goals.

In-person focus groups

A total of fifty-seven in-person focus groups were conducted across the country from November 2018 to June 2019. The groups included four types of research participants.

- Youth: Black, Hispanic, and white youth ages fifteen to twenty-one: forty-two focus groups total, with thirty-five among lower-income youth and seven among higher-income youth
- Young adults: Black, Hispanic, and white young adults ages twenty-six to twenty-nine: three focus groups
- Parents/guardians: Black, Hispanic, and white parents/guardians of youth ages fifteen to twenty-one: seven focus groups total, with four among lower-income and three among higher-income
- Adult influencers: Black, Hispanic, and white adults who work and/or volunteer with youth ages fifteen to twenty-one: five focus groups

Each focus group discussion was designed to be comprised of participants of the same race who did not know each other. Participants in younger youth groups (ages fifteen to twenty-one) were also of the same gender. Groups among adults were mixed-gender. There were generally six to nine participants in a group. Each group was moderated by an adult of the same race or ethnicity as the participants, and the conversations were always participant-driven.

Exceptions to this race-matched moderator approach described above were the two BUILD focus groups, which were mixed-race/ethnicity and mixed-gender and included some youth who knew one another, as well as having different adults moderate different portions of the discussions.

We intentionally structured the focus group moderator's discussion guide to ensure that youth felt comfortable sharing personal aspects of themselves. The moderators were highly-skilled professionals trained in the Heartwired approach to focus group moderation, which involves using deep listening skills and facilitating in a style that enables youth to open up.

Round 1 Focus Groups: The first round of in-person focus groups allowed us to better understand how key constituencies personally experience, or, in the case of adult participants, view, youth identity formation and its relation to education and work goals. We conducted thirty-four in-person focus groups from November 2018 to February 2019 in ten different locations (including rural and urban areas) in nine states: California, Colorado, Florida, Georgia, Illinois, Louisiana, Mississippi, New York, and Washington State. Twenty-five of the focus groups were conducted among Black, Hispanic, and lower-income white youth ages fifteen to twenty-one with a variety of career goals and life aspirations. Four of the groups were conducted among Black, Hispanic, and lower-income white parents or guardians of youth ages fifteen to twenty-one. Five of the groups were conducted among Black, Hispanic, and white adult influencers (people who work or volunteer with youth ages fifteen to twenty-one five or more hours per week).

Round 2 Focus Groups: The second round consisted of fifteen in-person focus groups conducted in May and June 2019 in six different locations (including urban and suburban areas) in California, Illinois, Maryland, and New York.

Two of these groups were conducted among lower-income Black youth (one male group, one female group) ages seventeen to twenty in Baltimore, Maryland. Seven additional groups were conducted among higher-income Black, Hispanic, and white youth ages seventeen to twenty in California, Illinois, Maryland, and New York. Three focus groups were also conducted among higher-income Black, Hispanic, and white parents of young people ages fifteen to twenty-one. These groups explored identity formation themes similar to the Round 1 groups and allowed us to better understand the differences that exist between how lower-income and higher-income youth form identity around education and work goals.

Three focus groups were also conducted among Black, Hispanic, and white young men and women ages twenty-six to twenty-nine who grew up in a lower-income household but are now middle- or higher-income. These groups, which were separated by race but were mixed-gender, provided an opportunity to look back on the identity formation process and identify key inflection points in young people's life pathways.

Intervention Focus Groups: We also conducted six Intervention focus groups in three locations in California (Downey, Oakland, and Sherman Oaks) in

June 2019 among Black, Hispanic, and lower-income white participants ages sixteen to eighteen. There were nine participants in each of these groups, and in addition to the larger adult-moderated group, discussion participants were also placed among peer-to-peer triads—sets of three participants of the same age—to generate small group discussions about each of their pathways. These groups explicitly explored themes related to social capital and allowed us to better understand how young people understand and value relationships in pursuance of their education and work goals.

BUILD Networking Focus Groups: Two focus groups—one in Los Angeles, the other in San Francisco, California—were conducted in conjunction with BUILD, an organization that uses entrepreneurial skills-building to empower students to pursue education and career (see https://build.org/about/). Participants were ages eighteen to twenty-two in Los Angeles and ages seventeen to eighteen in San Francisco; all groups were mixed-gender and included participants from a variety of racial and ethnic backgrounds. While not everyone in each location knew each other, participants were more familiar with each other in the BUILD groups compared to previous focus groups we conducted. Like the Intervention focus groups, these groups also explored reactions to and messaging around social capital. They also included three distinct components:

- a (much shorter) adult-moderated focus group;
- a social capital curriculum created and presented by BUILD staff; and
- a real-world opportunity to network with near-peer professionals in an informal, nonjudgmental setting.

ONLINE FOCUS GROUPS

We also conducted two multiday focus groups in late August 2019, with one group entirely in English and the other primarily in Spanish. Both groups included lower-income participants ages fifteen to twenty-one alongside some participants ages twenty-six to twenty-nine who grew up in lower-income households but are now middle- or higher-income.

In addition to exploring identity formation and education and work goals, the online focus groups allowed us to explore the roles information, advice, and support play in young people's lives, including information and advice from near-peers.

In the English-language group, there were a total of thirty participants from twelve states across the country: California, Colorado, Florida, Georgia, Illinois, Indiana, Louisiana, Michigan, New Mexico, New York, Pennsylvania, and Texas. There were a total of twelve Black participants (nine females, three males), nine Hispanic participants (six females, three males), and nine white participants (six females, three males). Fourteen of the participants had at least some college education.

In the Spanish-language group, there were a total of twenty-four participants from nine states across the country: California, Colorado, Florida, Georgia, Illinois, Kentucky, New Mexico, New York, and Texas. This group had thirteen Hispanic female and eleven Hispanic male participants, and nine had at least some college education.

QUALITATIVE FOCUS GROUP DISCUSSION STRUCTURE

With the exception of the BUILD and Intervention focus groups, the majority of the qualitative sessions among youth followed the structure summarized below. The parent and adult social influencer groups followed a similar structure with questions adjusted for adults. This summary shows the purpose for each section of the protocol, along with examples of the kinds of questions asked in each section.

I. Welcome/Introduction

Purpose: create a safe space; explain confidentiality and that discussions are strictly for research purposes; initial self-introductions by participants.

- All discussions are confidential and anonymous.
- You are encouraged to disagree/speak your mind; there are no right or wrong answers.
- If at any point you have any questions, ask.
- There is recording equipment (video/audiotape/camera for observers in other rooms, etc.).
- Participants are asked to introduce themselves (one at a time).
  - State your first name and age.
  - Who lives with you in your home? (Tell me a little about them.)
  - Tell me about school or work.

FIGURE A.1

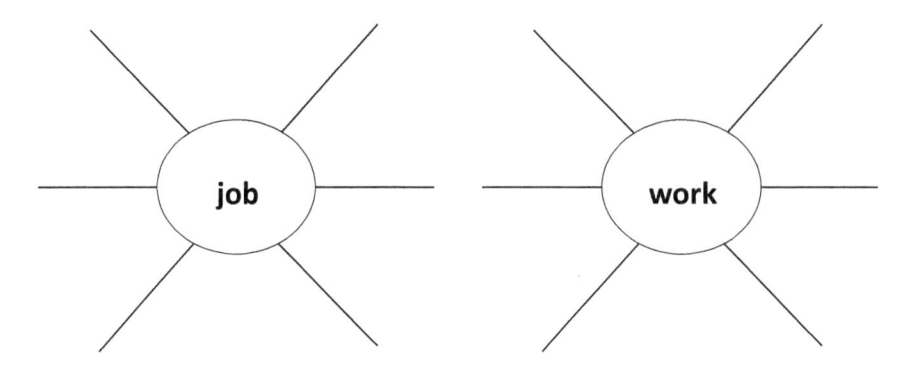

```
    \   |   /              \   |   /
     \  |  /                \  |  /
   ___( job )___         ___( work )___
      /  |  \               /  |  \
     /   |   \             /   |   \
```

II. Word Associations

Purpose: explore associations with job, work, and career; understand the language they personally use in discussing these subjects.

- On the lines or spokes coming out of each circle, please write down whatever words or phrases come to mind related to the word *job*. Anything that pops into your mind, whatever it is, write it down. Just like popcorn, a popcorn machine—whatever pops to mind. And then do the same with *work*.
- On this handout is another word: *career*. Just like before, please write down whatever words or phrases come to mind for you related to the word *career*. Anything that pops into your mind, whatever it is, write it down.

III. Self-Description

Purpose: understand how they identify themselves, both in general and/or as part of a racial, ethnic, or cultural group; mirror the language they use to describe themselves (e.g., Mexican, Latino, or Hispanic) throughout the remainder of the discussion.

- I want to know more about you and how you see yourself, how you would describe yourself. On the lines on this paper, please write down some of the words or phrases you would use to describe yourself.
- Now, here, please write down how you would describe your gender, race, ethnicity, culture, religion, or other parts of your background.
- What words did you write down to describe yourself?
- How did you describe your race, ethnicity, culture, religion, gender, or other parts of your background?

FIGURE A.2

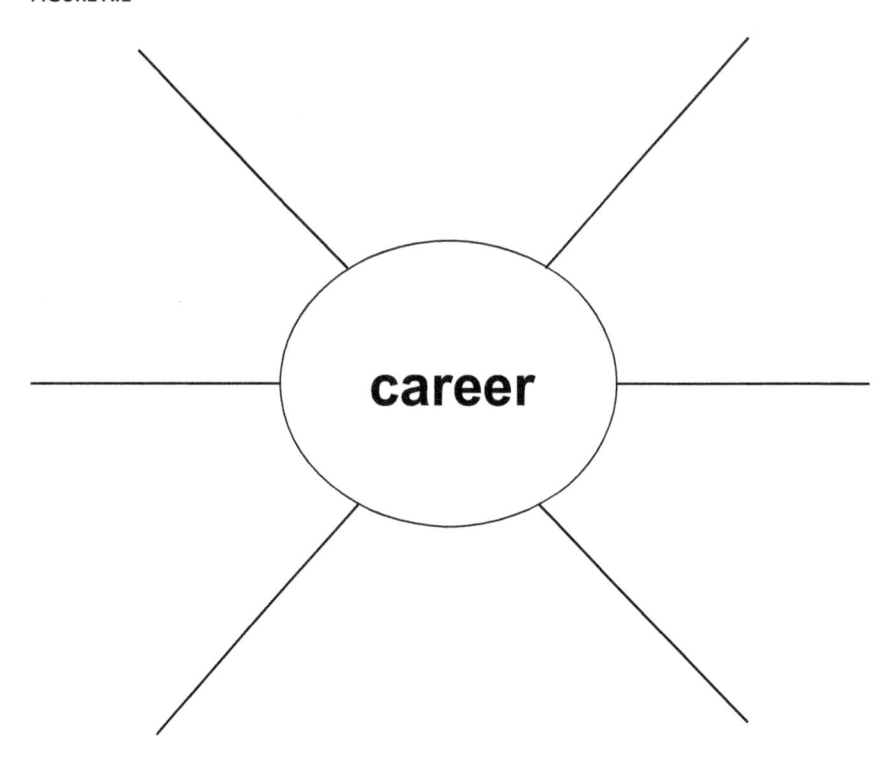

[Diagram: an oval labeled "career" with six lines radiating outward from it]

IV. Painting a Picture of Their Future

Purpose: bring the discussion back to work and then have them describe their futures at different ages.

- Imagine yourself when you are twenty-five years old. What is your life like? What are you doing? Where do you live? How do you spend your time? How do you make money? What is important to you? Paint a picture for me.
- What about when you are forty-five years old? Paint a picture for me. What is your life like? What are you doing? Where do you live? How do you spend your time? How do you make money? What is important to you?

V. Navigating the Path Toward Future Work

Purpose: explore in what ways they understand (or not) the pathways, opportunities, requirements, challenges to get themselves to the place(s) they want to be; in what ways they do or do not connect their own interests, strengths and lifestyle goals with what it takes to have the kind of job/work/career they would like to have; and explore their perceptions about the role of education/school in achieving their goals.

- On this handout is a curvy path with blank boxes that you can fill in—kind of like a game of life. Imagine that you are walking on this path. At one end of the path, write the kind of job, work, or career that you would like to do someday. That is your goal. Now write down where you are starting from. Now take a few minutes and fill in the spaces, describing how you might get from where you are now to where you want to be. What do you imagine are the steps or things that have to happen in order for you to get there? You can start anywhere. Feel free to include any things in your life that led you to where you are now.
- What are the specific things, experiences, knowledge, or people that you imagine would help you get there, to the end of your own pathway? Add those to your drawing—either in the boxes of your own personal path or outside the path.
- Tell me more about the kind of education, school, training, or certification you feel you might need during your pathway.
- Several of you have said *support* is important. Tell me about support—what does support look like? When someone is being supportive, what are they doing?
  - When someone is NOT being supportive, what does that look like? What are they doing that is not supportive?
- Take another look at this pathway you have written down. Take a moment to write down some of the barriers or challenges you might face. What are some things you might have to do, overcome, or avoid in order to stay on this pathway you've written down here?

VI. Influencers on Work Perspectives

Purpose: explore who influences their ideas about work and future, and in what ways.

- Are there people whose jobs you find interesting or that appeal to you?
  - Who are they?
  - What kind of work do they do, and what feels interesting for you about it?

- If you were to have a job that you feel is a *good job*, what words would you use to describe it? What about it makes it a *good job* for you?
  - Tell me what your ideal job, or work, or career would look like.
- If you were to have a job that you feel is a *bad job*, what words would you use to describe it? What about it makes it a *bad job* for you?

VII. Navigating Barriers Along the Way

Purpose: explore how they navigate structural barriers—including systemic racism, misogyny, stigma, and so—both personally and with advice from others.

- Thinking about how you described yourself earlier in our discussion, do you feel like your race or gender or ethnicity helps you, limits you, some of both, or has no real effect in terms of getting where you want to go in your life?
- Are there certain things you need to navigate, or things you have to manage—deal with—in certain ways?
- How do you do that?

VIII. Self-Efficacy and Belonging

Purpose: understand how they perceive their own strengths and weaknesses and the alignment of those qualities with the kind of work they like or dislike. In this section, we expect that the youth will reference teachers/school or other education-related experiences. If they do not, we will probe it.

- What are the things that you enjoy? What are the things that you feel you are really good at, that you have as strengths?
- Now focusing on friends and family . . . Are there people in your life who tell you that you are good at *this* or *that*, that you have *this* or *that* as a strength? People who build you up?
- What are the things that you feel you are not so good at, things that are harder for you or that you feel you don't do as well at?
- Now thinking just about your friends . . . Do you feel that your friends help you to accomplish your own personal goals, get in the way of you accomplishing your goals, or that they don't really have an impact on that one way or another?
- Thinking about your family . . . Do you feel that your family is helping you to accomplish your own personal goals, gets in the way of you accomplishing your goals, or that they don't really have an impact on that one way or another?

- Now let me ask you . . . Generally, do you feel that you have people in your life—family, friends, teachers, other people—who have their own goals, expectations, hopes for you—or not really?

IX. Conclusion

Purpose: identify which aspects of the discussion are most prominent or important for the participants.

- We've talked a lot. When you are headed home, what will you be thinking about from our discussion? What will be on your mind, what will you be wondering about?

QUALITATIVE ANALYSIS

To aid our in-depth analysis of the qualitative data, we video recorded each focus group discussion and created a detailed transcript of each two-hour conversation. In addition, we transcribed the hand-written entries from handout exercises—for example, the word association exercises and the self-descriptions participants wrote down—conducted during each discussion. Furthermore, we produced an extensive quote library (more than five-hundred pages) containing illustrative quotes from the focus group participants organized into thematic areas.

We then used these qualitative resources to conduct an in-depth analysis, using team and advisory team meetings to share observations, suggest hypotheses, consider implications, and make meaning of the data. Importantly, our analysis took place iteratively as the focus group discussions progressed to ensure our analysis and corresponding hypotheses evolved to reflect our latest thinking.

ONLINE SURVEY

We conducted an online nationwide survey in September 2019 that integrated and expanded upon our qualitative findings from the focus groups. The survey was conducted among 3,545 young people ages fifteen to twenty-one and includes:

- 495 white females and 583 white males
- 486 Black females and 451 Black males
- 499 Hispanic females and 398 Hispanic males

- 158 Asian Pacific Islander females and 146 Asian Pacific Islander males
- 26 Native American females and 23 Native American males
- 109 females and 46 males who identify with two or more ethnic groups

This survey helped to quantify the qualitative results and allowed us to further explore issues of identity formation and education and work goals and refine our findings, especially as they pertain to race and gender.

APPENDIX B

Worksheet: Mapping Life and Career Pathways with Young People

Striving to Thriving researchers developed a pathways worksheet in which focus group participants identified a life or career goal and mapped out the steps and stages they believed they might initiate or pass through as they pursued those goals. After completing the worksheet, participants were asked to narrate their pathway for the group and describe both the supports they thought they would need and the challenges they believed they might encounter or experience, as well as whether and how they believed they might overcome those challenges.

The following guidance was previously published as part of the Designing Pathways with Young People Toolkit available at https://equitablefutures.org.

STEP 1. INTRODUCE THE ACTIVITY

Print one worksheet for every young person in your group. Set out colored markers and regular writing pens for each person. Introduce the activity and be transparent about why you are doing the exercise.

You may consider using or adapting the following script:

- *In this activity, you will explore your goals and imagine the steps you might take to get there.*
- *On this worksheet is a curvy path with blank boxes that you can fill in—kind of like a game of life.*
- *Imagine that you are walking on this path. At one end of the path, write the kind of job, work, or career that you would like to do someday. That is your goal.*
- *Now write down where you are starting from. You can start anywhere.*

STEP 2. EXPLORE STEPS, STAGES, AND EXPERIENCES

Once all participants in the group have had an opportunity to write down their starting point and their goal(s), ask them to fill in the spaces (steps, stages, and experiences) in between.

You may consider using or adapting the following script:

- *Now take a few minutes and fill in the spaces that describe how you might get from where you are now to where you want to be.*
- *Feel free to include any things in your life that led you to where you are now. If you wish, you can use the colored pens as well as the pen provided.*
- *What do you imagine are the steps, stages, or experiences that have to happen in order for you to get there?*
- *What supports or resources will you need to move successfully through your pathway and reach your goals?*

Follow-up prompts:

After the group has had a few minutes to work independently, you may choose to follow up with the following prompts, or you can design your own based on what you want to learn about young people's experiences or future aspirations. Encourage them to write inside or outside of the boxes as they continue to respond to your prompts and add detail to their pathway.

- *What kind of education, school, training, or certification do you feel you might need along your pathway?*
- *What kinds of people will you meet along the way? What role will each person play?*

STEP 3. IDENTIFY CHALLENGES AND BARRIERS

When you can see that the group has responded to your earlier prompts and the worksheets are beginning to look full and rich with detail, you can ask young people about the challenges and barriers they have already experienced or anticipate experiencing as they make their way toward their goal(s).

You may consider using or adapting the following script:

- *Now take a few minutes and consider the barriers or challenges you might face in order to reach your goals. What are the things you might have to avoid or overcome to stay on your pathway and get to your goal(s)?*

Suggested follow-up prompts:

- *What do you imagine will be the resources, information, or supports you will need to overcome these challenges/barriers?*
- *Are there specific people who you think will play an important role in your success?*

After the group has responded to these final prompts, give them a minute or so to review their pathway and add any finishing touches before putting down their pens.

STEP 4. SHARE WITH PEERS

Go around the room and ask the participants to share their pathway with the full group. While sharing, they should talk through their full pathway by holding it up so everyone can see it or by walking the group through each step. For example, a young person may share: "My goal is x. I put myself here because I am currently in high school. The next step is y. I will need to learn z in order to do y." You can find example pathways and pathway narratives in the *Striving to Thriving* report, available at https://www.equitablefutures.org.

After the participants describe their pathways, you may choose to probe specific ideas or concepts. We recommend reflecting young people's own language as you construct probes or discussion questions (e.g., if they use the term *racism*, use this term instead of *discrimination* or *bias*).

Some examples of ideas or concepts that may come up in discussion include the following:

- **Support.** *Young people often use the word* support *to describe the role of people in their lives, but this word means different things to different people. Ask what kind of support they think they will need and who can or will provide that? Where might they look for that support?*
- **Discrimination and bias.** *Young people often feel that their racial, ethnic, cultural, or gender identity will benefit them as they move toward their future goals. Many also worry about discrimination and bias. It may be important to learn more about what systemic inequalities they expect to experience and how they believe this may impact their trajectories.*

- **Entrepreneurship.** *Many young people feel positively about the prospect of doing their own thing or owning their own business, being their own boss, or having a side hustle.*
- **Thriving.** *Most young people see themselves thriving in their future lives. They are excited to talk about the way they imagine their lives unfolding and how it will feel to achieve their goals—the kind of life they want to live and the quality of life that they feel is most important. In many cases, young people are motivated by the life they imagine living and less by the type of work they imagine doing.*

Using this activity in a group or individual context

This activity was originally developed for use in groups of six to eight young people moderated by a neutral adult who helped to facilitate the presentation of each pathway and the discussion that followed. However, the activity can also be conducted with one young person responding to one adult or in a small group discussion between near-peers and peers. In a small group context, researchers found that it was beneficial to involve young people with a diversity of aspirations and goals, including young people whose goals are more and less clearly defined. Researchers heard from young people that they appreciated the opportunity to be in conversation with peers they perceive to be different from them, and they also valued opportunities to both learn from and teach their peers.

STEP 5. REFLECTIONS AND APPRECIATIONS

After all the young people have shared their pathways, and you've had a chance to explore specific themes or ideas that they raise, consider bringing the group together to reflect on their experience doing the pathway activity.

You might consider the following reflection questions:

- *As your peers were sharing, what did you hear? What stands out to you?*
- *Did you learn anything new about yourself or others? If so, what?*
- *What is your overall takeaway from this?*
- *We've talked about a lot today. What are you left thinking about? What are you curious about or left wondering?*
- *What questions do you have?*
- *Thank the group for sharing their thinking and their aspirations with you and their peers and then end the activity.*

You may want to consider periodically checking back in with the young people from this group to revisit their pathways worksheets. You can ask additional reflection questions to help young people assess how they are moving along their pathway, as well as how their experiences in your program might be helping them achieve their life goals.

Notes

Series Editor Foreword
1. Robert Schwartz and Rachel Lipson, eds., *America's Hidden Economic Engines* (Cambridge, MA: Harvard Education Press, 2023).
2. Nancy Hoffman and Robert Schwartz, *Learning for Careers: The Pathways to Prosperity Network* (Cambridge, MA: Harvard Education Press, 2017); and Marc S. Tucker, ed., *Vocational Education and Training for a Global Economy: Lessons from Four Countries* (Cambridge, MA: Harvard Education Press, 2019).
3. Robert Halpern, *Youth, Education, and the Role of Society* (Cambridge, MA: Harvard Education Press, 2013).
4. Halpern, *Youth, Education, and the Role of Society*, 4.
5. Halpern, *Youth, Education, and the Role of Society*, 25.
6. Jessica Callahan et al., *Influences on Occupational Identity in Adolescence: A Review of Research and Programs* (Irvine, CA: Connected Learning Alliance, 2019), https://clalliance.org/wp-content/uploads/2019/05/Influences_on_Occupational_Identity_Adolescence.pdf.

Preface
1. *Striving to Thriving: Occupational Identity Formation among Black and Hispanic Young People and Young People from Lower-Income Households*, https://www.equitablefutures.org/wp-content/uploads/2021/09/Striving-to-Thriving-Full-Report-October-2020.pdf.

Introduction
1. Amy K. Marks, G. Alice Woolverton, and Cynthia García Coll, "Risk and Resilience in Minority Youth Populations," *Annual Review of Clinical Psychology*, vol. 16 (2020): 151–63.
2. "Storytelling for Impact MAT Access Project," Communication Training Series, webinar video, presented by Fig and Sass, Seattle, WA, May 2024; "Racial Narrative Theory," Trevor Smith, accessed October 27, 2024, https://trevorsmith.com/about-3.
3. "Narrative Tech: Categories, needs and what's next," Narrative Initiative, December 6, 2019, https://www.narrativeinitiative.org/post/narrative-tech-categories-needs-and-what-s-next.
4. Rashad Robinson, "*Changing Our Narrative About Narrative,*" Othering & Belonging Institute, April 18, 2018, https://belonging.berkeley.edu/changing-our-narrative-about-narrative.
5. Silvia Edling, "Between Curriculum Complexity and Stereotypes: Exploring Stereotypes of Teachers and Education in Media as a Question of Structural Violence," *Journal of Curriculum Studies* 47, no. 3 (2014): 399–415.
6. *Striving to Thriving: Occupational Identity Formation among Black and Hispanic Young People and Young People from Lower-Income Households*, https://www.equitablefutures.org/wp-content/uploads/2021/09/Striving-to-Thriving-Full-Report-October-2020.pdf.

7. Luis Noe-Bustamante, Lauren Mora, and Mark Hugo Lopez, *About One-in-Four U.S. Hispanics Have Heard of Latinx, but Just 3% Use It* (Washington, DC: Pew Research Center's Hispanic Trends Project, 2020), https://www.pewresearch.org/hispanic/2020/08/11/about-one-in-four-u-s-hispanics-have-heard-of-latinx-but-just-3-use-it.
8. For a study on how discrimination is continuously resisted and managed by Black youth, see Eleanor K. Seaton and Masumi Iida, "Racial Discrimination and Racial Identity: Daily Moderation among Black Youth," *American Psychologist* 74, no. 1 (2019): 117–27, https://doi.org/10.1037/amp0000367. For a poignant and powerful study of how mothers of Black sons shape these self-narratives, see Sohini Das et al., "Lessons of Resistance from Black Mothers to their Black Sons," *Journal of Research on Adolescents* 32, no. 3 (2022): 981–98, https://doi.org/10.1111/jora.12740. See also Ciara S. Glover, Aisha Walker, and Josefina Bañales, "Engagement Coping Responses to Adolescents' Negative Racialized Experiences," *Journal of Research on Adolescence* 32, no. 1 (2022): 134–50, https://doi.org/10.1111/jora.12727. For an empirical case of a sociolinguistic approach, see Stanton Wortham, "Representation and Enactment in Autobiographical Narrative," in *Theoretical Psychology: Critical Contributions*, ed. Niamh Stephenson, H. L. Radtke, R. J. Jorna, and Henderikus J. Stam (Concord, ON: Captus Press, 2001), 258–66.
9. This phrase "occupational identity" is defined in Jessica Callahan, Mizuko Ito, Rea Campbell, and Stephen and Amanda Wortman, "Influences on Occupational Identity in Adolescence: A Review of Research and Programs" (Irvine, CA: Connected Learning Alliance, 2019), https://clalliance.org/wp-content/uploads/2019/05/Influences_on_Occupational_Identity_Adolescence.pdf, p. 4.
10. Robert Pérez and Amy Simon, *Heartwired: Human Behavior, Strategic Opinion Research and the Audacious Pursuit of Social Change* (Oakland, CA: Goodwin Simon Strategic Research, 2017), https://heartwiredforchange.com/wp-content/uploads/2019/04/Heartwired-Apr12-digital.pdf.
11. Melanie C. Green and Marc Sestir, "Transportation Theory," in *The International Encyclopedia of Media Effects*, ed. P. Rössler, C. A. Hoffner and L. Zoonen (Chichester, UK: Wiley, 2017), 1–14, https://doi.org/10.1002/9781118783764.wbieme0083; and Dan R. Johnson, "Transportation into a Story Increases Empathy, Prosocial Behavior, and Perceptual Bias toward Fearful Expressions," *Personality and Individual Differences* 52, no. 2 (2012): 150–55, https://doi.org/10.1016/j.paid.2011.10.005.
12. *Striving to Thriving: Occupational Identity Formation among Black and Hispanic Young People and Young People from Lower-Income Households*, https://www.equitablefutures.org/wp-content/uploads/2021/09/Striving-to-Thriving-Full-Report-October-2020.pdf.
13. For a broad introduction to the concept of "identity" in the social sciences, see P. L. Hammack, "Theoretical Foundations of Identity," in *The Oxford Handbook of Identity Development*, ed. Kate C. McLean and Moin Syed (Oxford: Oxford University Press, 2015), 11–30. For a very helpful delineation of the potential pitfalls of using "identity" in sociocultural analysis, see Rogers Brubaker and Frederick Cooper, "Beyond 'Identity,'" *Theory and Society* 29, no. 1 (2000): 1–47, http://www.jstor.org/stable/3108478.
14. See the following sources on how racial and ethnic minority youth exert agency over their stories amid discrimination: Limarys Caraballo, "Being 'Loud': Identities-in-Practice in a Figured World of Achievement," *American Educational Research Journal* 56, no. 4 (2019): 1281–317, https://doi.org/10.3102/0002831218816059; Dorinda Carter, "Achievement as Resistance: The Development of a Critical Race Achievement Ideology among Black Achievers," *Harvard Educational Research Review* 78, no. 3 (2008): 466–97, https://doi.org

/10.17763/haer.78.3.83138829847hw844; Danielle Macias and Maura Shramko, "Counterstory Methodology in a University-High School Collaboration to Center and Humanize Latina/o Voices," *Journal of Community Psychology* 49, no. 5 (2021): 1436–56, https://doi.org/10.1002/jcop.22496; and Leoandra O. Rogers and Niobe Way, "Reimagining Social and Emotional Development: Accommodation and Resistance to Dominant Ideologies in the Identities and Friendships of Boys of Color," *Human Development* 61, no. 6 (2018): 311–31, https://www.jstor.org/stable/26765223.

Chapter 1

1. For a fairly recent relevant study from the originator of the term "self-efficacy," Albert Bandura, see Albert Bandura et al., "Self-Efficacy Beliefs as Shapers of Children's Aspirations and Career Trajectories," *Child Development* 72, no. 1 (2001): 187–206, https://doi.org/10.1111/1467-8624.00273. For an analysis of the cultivation of critical consciousness among adolescents, see Corine P. Tyler et al., "Critical Consciousness in Late Adolescence: Understanding If, How, and Why Youth Act," *Journal of Applied Developmental Psychology* 70 (2020): 101–65, https://doi.org/10.1016/j.appdev.2020.101165.
2. For a concise and useful overview of agency theory, widely applicable yet focused on linguistic anthropological methodologies, see Laura M. Ahearn, "Agency," *Journal of Linguistic Anthropology* 9, no. 1/2 (1999): 12–15. For a recent critique of the analytical uses of agency as a term of art, see Julia Coffey and David Farrugia, "Unpacking the Black Box: The Problem of Agency in the Sociology of Youth," *Journal of Youth Studies* 17, no. 4 (2013): 461–74, https://doi.org/10.1080/13676261.2013.830707.
3. On supporting young women and girls of color's agency, see Katie Clonan-Roy, Charlotte E. Jacobs, and Michael J. Nakkula, "Towards a Model of Positive Youth Development Specific to Girls of Color: Perspectives on Development, Resilience, and Empowerment," *Gender Issues* 33, no. 2 (2016): 96–121, https://doi.org/10.1007/s12147-016-9156-7; see also Jennifer D. Turner and Autumn A. Griffin, "Brown Girls Dreaming: Adolescent Black Girls' Futuremaking through Multimodal Representations of Race, Gender, and Career Aspirations," *Research in the Teaching of English* 55, no. 2 (2020): 109–33, https://doi.org/10.58680/rte202031020; and Uma M. Jayakumar, Rican Vue, and Walter Allen, "Pathways to College for Young Black Scholars: A Community Cultural Wealth Perspective," *Harvard Educational Review* 83, no. 4 (2013): 551–79, https://doi.org/10.17763/haer.83.4.4k1mq00162433l28.
4. Gabriel's pathway exercise is not included in the book. A reproduction of his pathway was not available at the time of print.
5. See Eleanor K. Seaton and Masumi Iida, "Racial Discrimination and Racial Identity: Daily Moderation among Black Youth," *American Psychologist* 74, no. 1 (2019): 117–27.
6. An influential text on student autonomy is Meira Levinson, *The Demands of Liberal Education* (Oxford: Oxford University Press, 1999). On child rights broadly, see Kate Butler, *Child Rights: The Movement, International Law, and Opposition* (West Lafayette, IN: Purdue University Press, 2012). On applying a child rights and a social justice approach to school counseling, see Shereen C. Naser et al., "Using Child Rights Education to Infuse a Social Justice Framework into Universal Programming," *School Psychology International* 41, no. 1 (2019): 13–36, https://doi.org/10.1177/0143034319894363.
7. *Striving to Thriving: Occupational Identity Formation among Black and Hispanic Young People and Young People from Lower-Income Households*, https://www.equitablefutures.org/wp-content/uploads/2021/09/Striving-to-Thriving-Full-Report-October-2020.pdf.

Chapter 2

1. Maurice O. Wallace, *Constructing the Black Masculine: Identity and Ideality in African American Men's Literature and Culture, 1775–1995* (Duke University Press, 2002): 1–15; Michelle Alexander, *The New Jim Crow: Mass Incarceration in the Age of Colorblindness* (London: Penguin Books, 2019): 242–45.
2. For a recent summative analysis of this topic, see Suneal Kolluri and Antar A. Tichavakunda, "The Counter-Deficit Lens in Educational Research: Interrogating Conceptions of Structural Oppression," *Review of Educational Research* 93, no. 5 (2022): 641–78, https://doi.org/10.3102/00346543221125225.
3. Leoandra O. Rogers and Niobe Way, "Reimagining Social and Emotional Development: Accommodation and Resistance to Dominant Ideologies in the Identities and Friendships of Boys of Color," *Human Development* 61, no. 6 (2018): 311–31, https://www.jstor.org/stable/26765223. See also, on the general topic of masculinities, Michael Di Bianca and James R. Mahalik, "A Relational-Cultural Framework for Promoting Healthy Masculinities," *American Psychologist* 77, no. 3 (2022): 321–32, https://doi.org/10.1037/amp0000929. On Black youth masculinities in school settings from an ethnographic perspective, see Quaylan Allen, "'They Write Me Off and Don't Give Me a Chance to Learn Anything': Positioning, Discipline, and Black Masculinities in School," *Anthropology & Education Quarterly* 48, no. 3 (2017): 269–83, https://doi.org/10.1111/aeq.12199.
4. For connections between resisting neoliberalist ideology and Black youth empowerment, see Bianca J. Baldridge, "'It's like this Myth of the Supernegro': Resisting Narratives of Damage and Struggle in the Neoliberal Educational Policy Context," *Race Ethnicity and Education* 20, no. 6 (2016): 781–95.

Chapter 3

1. A self-tape is a video an actor takes of themselves reading the lines to a specific part or role. This self-tape is submitted to a director or casting agent and, if successful, the actor is invited to read the part in person or with another actor.
2. Nancy E. Hill and Alexis Redding, *The End of Adolescence: The Lost Art of Delaying Adulthood* (Cambridge, MA: Harvard University Press, 2021), 3.
3. Barbara Schneider and David Stevenson, *The Ambitious Generation: America's Teenagers Motivated But Directionless* (New Haven, CT: Yale University Press, 1999), 107.
4. David Williamson Shaffer, Wesley Collier, and A. R. Ruis, "A Tutorial on Epistemic Network Analysis: Analyzing the Structure of Connections in Cognitive, Social, and Interaction Data," *Journal of Learning Analytics* 3, no. 3 (2016): 9–45, https://doi.org/10.18608/jla.2016.33.3; see also Epistemic Network Analysis website, https://www.epistemicnetwork.org/.
5. For connections to the mythos of the meritocratic "American Dream," see David T. Lardier et al., "Merit in Meritocracy: Uncovering the Myth of Exceptionality and Self-Reliance through the Voices of Urban Youth of Color," *Education and Urban Society* 51, no. 4 (2019): 474–500, https://doi.org/10.1177/0013124517727583. For a perspective from narrative sociolinguistics, see Anna De Fina, "What Is Your Dream? Fashioning the Migrant Self," *Language & Communication* 59 (2018): 42–52, https://doi.org/10.1016/j.langcom.2017.02.002. For a critical postcolonial perspective, see this section introduction regarding youth development in African contexts: Andrew Babson, "African Youth Development: Claiming the Past for the Future in Neoliberal Times," in *Adolescent Psychology in Today's World: Global Perspectives on Risk, Relationships, and Development: Volume 3, Africa, Asia and the Middle East*, ed. Andrew Schneider-Muñoz and Michael Nakkula (Westport, CT: Praeger, 2018), 1–24.

Chapter 4

1. Chicago Beyond, *Why Am I Always Being Researched?* (Chicago, IL: Chicago Beyond, 2018), https://wp.chicagobeyond.org/wp-content/uploads/2023/09/ChicagoBeyond_Why-Am-I.pdf.
2. Equitable Futures, *Striving to Thriving: Occupational Identity Formation among Black and Hispanic Young People and Young People from Households with Lower Incomes* (New York, NY: Equitable Futures, 2020), https://equitablefutures.org/wp-content/uploads/2021/08/Striving-to-Thriving-Report-in-Brief-Sept-2020-Updated.pdf.
3. Edwin Rios, "US schools remain highly segregated by race and class, analysis shows," The Guardian, July 15, 2022, https://www.theguardian.com/education/2022/jul/15/us-schools-segregated-race-class-analysis#:~:text=While%20Black%20students%20accounted%20for,double%20that%20of%20Black%20students.
4. Leoandra O. Rogers and Niobe Way, "Reimagining Social and Emotional Development: Accommodation and Resistance to Dominant Ideologies in the Identities and Friendships of Boys of Color," *Human Development* 61, no. 6 (2018): 311–31, https://www.jstor.org/stable/26765223. See also, on the general topic of masculinities, Michael Di Bianca and James R. Mahalik, "A Relational-Cultural Framework for Promoting Healthy Masculinities," *American Psychologist* 77, no. 3 (2022): 321–32, https://doi.org/10.1037/amp0000929. On Black youth masculinities in school settings from an ethnographic perspective, see Quaylan Allen, "'They Write Me Off and Don't Give Me a Chance to Learn Anything': Positioning, Discipline, and Black Masculinities in School," *Anthropology & Education Quarterly* 48, no. 3 (2017): 269–83, https://doi.org/10.1111/aeq.12199.

Chapter 5

1. The acronym CTE is derived from a previous name in which the organization included the words "computer, technical, education"; see Advance CTE, *With Learners, Not for Learners: A Toolkit for Elevating Learner Voice in CTE* (Silver Spring, MD: Advance CTE, 2023), https://careertech.org/resource/learner-voice-toolkit; see Informed Change and Hamai Consulting, *Powered by Youth Voice: Future Directions for Afterschool*, https://www.everyhourcounts.org/youthengagement.
2. Equitable Futures, https://equitablefutures.org.
3. Equitable Futures, "Designing Pathways with Young People," toolkit, https://www.equitablefutures.org/toolkit/designing-pathways-with-young-people.
4. BUILD Inc, empowers young people with entrepreneurial skills-building to help them achieve their career and life goals; see BUILD website, https://build.org/about/.
5. Natalie Fotias, "The Power of Asset Framing: A Conversation with Trabian Shorters," *The Skillman Foundation Blog*, September 24, 2018, https://www.skillman.org/blog/the-power-of-asset-framing.
6. Jessica Callahan et al., *Influences on Occupational Identity in Adolescence: A Review of Research and Programs* (Irvine, CA: Connected Learning Alliance, 2019), https://clalliance.org/wp-content/uploads/2019/05/Influences_on_Occupational_Identity_Adolescence.pdf.
7. This guidance was previously published as a worksheet in the "Designing Pathways with Young People" toolkit.
8. Gerald R. Adams and Sheila K. Marshall, "A Developmental Social Psychology of Identity: Understanding the Person-in-Context," *Journal of Adolescence* 19, no. 5 (1996): 429–42, https://doi.org/10.1006/jado.1996.0041.

9. R. E. H. Muuss, Eli Velder, and Harriet Porton, eds., "Erik Erikson's Theory of Identity Development," in *Theories of Adolescence* (New York, NY: McGraw-Hill, 1996), 42–57.
10. Mary E. Arnold, "Supporting Adolescent Exploration and Commitment: Identity Formation, Thriving, and Positive Youth Development," *Journal of Youth Development* 12, no. 4 (2017): 1–15, https://doi.org/10.5195/jyd.2017.522.
11. Callahan et al., *Influences on Occupational Identity in Adolescence*, 7.
12. Junior Achievement and The Hartford, *Insuring Career Success: Teen Perceptions of Career Selection* (Hartford, CT: The Hartford, 2018), https://centraliowa.ja.org/dA/5f6fee1879/criticalIssuePdfDocument/JA%20Hartford%20White%20Paper%20rev.pdf?language_id=1, 2018; and Peter Akosah-Twumasi et al., "A Systematic Review of Factors That Influence Youths Career Choices: The Role of Culture, *Secondary Educational Psychology*, July 18, 2018, https://www.frontiersin.org/articles/10.3389/feduc.2018.00058/full.
13. Douglas Broom, "Having Many Careers Will Be the Norm, Experts Say," *World Economic Forum: Forum Institutional*, May 2, 2023, https://www.weforum.org/agenda/2023/05/workers-multiple-careers-jobs-skills.
14. Acceptance can be positive when young people embrace a job or career that matches their interests, strengths, likes and dislikes, and personal goals. Acceptance can also be a type of settling when young people do not have access to a diversity of examples of jobs and careers, and so believe what they see is all there is. They lack access to other options or cannot envision those other options as relevant or accessible to them.

About the Author

Michaela Leslie-Rule is a researcher, artist, and cultural strategist. For more than two decades, she has supported movement, nonprofit, and philanthropic leaders to advance racial and gender justice by leveraging the power of stories. She has partnered with communities in the United States, Europe, and East and Central Africa to learn about and make progress on a range of issues, including gender-based violence, maternal-child health, K–12 education, career pathways for young people, and reproductive justice. Michaela is a founding member of the Spiritual Technologies Project, a collaboration between composers, musicians, and other culture bearers exploring the knowledge held by Black communities in the American South. She also co-developed the Emmy-nominated *Fundamental* film series, produced by the Global Fund for Women and directed by Sharmeen Obaid Chinoy. She lives with her family in Seattle.

Index

achievement continuum, 87
adults
    assumptions of, 56
    elevating youth voice over, 85–86, 91–93, 96, 110
    limited interaction with young people, 9–10
agency of youth, 95, 105
Ali
    barriers for, 67
    on careers, 48, 49
    introduction of, 42
    on jobs, 45
    on parent's guidance, 45
    on racism, 69
    reflections on focus group, 82
    on thriving, 74
"all up to them," 67
assessment, 101, 106
asset-based narrative, 66, 94–95
assumptions of adults, 56

barriers to success, 66–67
Black young people, 1–4, 40, 43–50, 93–94. *See also specific focus group participants*
bold text, meaning of, 16
bracketed text, meaning of, 16
BUILD Inc., 93

Callahan, Jessica, 102–103
careers. *See also* jobs; work
    assumptions of adults about, 56
    change of over life, 72, 104
    focus group view of, 48–50
    framing as terminal rather than iterative, 108
categorization of people, x, 4–6, 99
Cedric
    on careers, 48, 49
    introduction of, 42
    on jobs, 44
    nonlinearity of striving, 71
    on parent's guidance, 45
    pathway for, 57–59
    reflections on focus group, 82, 83
    self-description, 68
    on work, 46
change, transformative, 90
college degrees, not used by people in their employment, 45, 62–63
crisis and commitment, 101
crisis narrative, 1–4, 93–94

data aggregation, ix
day jobs, 44–45. *See also* jobs
deficit narrative, 66, 71
Designing Pathways with Young People toolkit, 92
discrimination. *See* racism
dominant narratives, defined, 2
dreams, valuing all, 73–74
dropouts, 45

engagement versus participation, 102–103
entry-level jobs, 44–45
epistemic network analysis (ENA), 71
Equitable Futures, 92
Erickson, Erik, 101

exploration, 102, 107. *See also Exposure, Exploration, and Selection* framework
exposure, 105–106. *See also Exposure, Exploration, and Selection* framework
Exposure, Engagement, and Participation framework, 102–103
Exposure, Exploration, and Selection framework, 97, 101–109
extracurricular programs, homogeneity of, 87–88

financial concerns as barrier, 67
Five Occupational Pathways framework
 creation of, 52–53
 how to use, 65–66, 98–101
 knowing what they want and how to get there, 54–62
 limits of, 53
 myths about, 71–75
 not classification system, x, 99
 not sure what they want but have idea of exploration steps, 62–66
 overview, 97–101
 purpose of, 97
focus groups. *See also specific participants by name*
 all participants impacted by, 88–89
 as extractive, 77
 formation of, 41
 heterogeneity of, 78, 86–89
 as intervention, 84
 lifts given by members of, 78–81, 83
 as meaningful conversations, 77–78
 settings for, 17–18, 41–42
 setup and ground rules for, 86
 unintended impacts of, x, 8–9, 82–84
fresh starts, 19–20
fulfillment, careers offering, 48–49

Gabriel, 26–29, 34, 35, 36
generalizations about young people, as inaccurate, 9–10
goals, valuing all, 73–74
good life, good job necessary for, 36–37, 72

Halpern, Robert, xi–xii
Heartwired methodology, 7
heterogeneity of groups, 78, 86–89
Hispanic young people, crisis narrative about, 1–4
homogeneity of groups, 87–88
human development theories, 101

immersion with young people, 10–12, 13–17
individuals. *See also* voices
 categories versus, 4–6
 listening to rather than seeing as group, 13–17, 74–75, 97
 responsibility as burden on, 34–36
italicized text, meaning of, 15–16

jobs. *See also* careers; work
 careers compared, 49–50
 as entry point to opportunity, 47
 focus group view of, 44–45
 school as, 58
 work compared, 46–47

Lamar
 introduction of, 42
 on jobs, 44
 pathway for, 59–62
 on racism, 69, 70
 reflections on focus group, 82, 83
 self-description, 68
 on thriving, 74
 on work, 47–48
language, occupational, 43–50
language choice for self-descriptions, 95

Latinx, as word choice, 5
lifts given by group members, 78–81, 83
listening, importance of, 13–17, 74–75, 97
lived experience, devaluation of those of young people, 5–6
lower-income young people, crisis narrative about, 1–4
Lukas
  barriers for, 67
  on careers, 49
  introduction of, 42
  on jobs, 44–45
  overview, 62–65
  reflections on focus group, 82
  self-description, 68
Lyrik
  barriers for, 67
  on careers, 48, 49
  dreams of, 34
  introduction of, 42
  lifts for, 79
  nonlinearity of striving, 71
  overview, 29–32
  pathway for, 29–32, 36
  on racism, 69, 70
  responsibility as burden on, 35

Malcolm
  on careers, 48, 49
  introduction of, 42
  lifts by, 79–81
  pathway for, 80–81
  on racism, 69
  self-description, 68
  on thriving, 74
  on work, 46, 47
Maria, 22–26, 34, 35, 36
Miles, 42, 44, 83
moderator role, 85–86
money as barrier, 67
mutuality, embedding, 95–96

narratives
  asset-based, 66, 94–95
  of author, 89–90
  crisis narrative, 1–4, 93–94
  deficit narrative, 66, 71
  defined, 2
  power of, 2, 40
  of racism versus self-perception of, 68–71
  radically new needed, 90
network building, 64–65
nonlinearity of striving, 66, 71–75, 108–109

occupational identity development, 64, 101–109. *See also Five Occupational Pathways* framework; pathways; striving; *Surviving, Striving, and Thriving* framework
occupational language, 43–50

paradox of Black men, 40
participation versus engagement, 102–103
pathways. *See also Five Occupational Pathways* framework; striving; visual pathways
  barriers to, 66–67
  Gabriel, 36
  Lamar, 59–62
  Lyrik, 29–32, 36
  Malcolm, 80–81
  Maria, 25, 36
  Renee, 21, 36
  Xavier, 54–57

racism
  as barrier, 67, 69–70
  Lyrik and, 32
  Maria and, 24
  narrative of versus self-perception of, 68–71

relationship building
  heterogeneity of groups and, 88
  by Lamar, 61–62
  by Lukas, 64–65
  mutuality, embedding, 95–96
  by Xavier, 56–57
  Renee, 18–22, 34, 35, 36
  research design, 6–9, 84–90, 93

schools, xi–xii, 58
segregation, 87–88
selection, 103, 107–108. *See also Exposure, Exploration, and Selection* framework
self-efficacy, 47
self-perception, 68–71
Simon, Amy, 7
society as barrier, 67
stories, xvii–xviii, 2, 40
strength narrative, 66, 94–95
striving. *See also Five Occupational Pathways* framework; *Surviving, Striving, and Thriving* framework
  defined, 33
  nonlinearity of, 66, 71–75, 108–109
  as occupational pathway building, 50
  overview, 50, 51–52
  stepping stones for, 53–54
  work as, 46
Striving to Thriving research project, 7, 10, 84–90, 91–93
surviving, 33, 43, 46. *See also Surviving, Striving, and Thriving* framework
Surviving, Striving, and Thriving framework, 32–34, 42–43, 96. *See also* striving; surviving; thriving
systems, individual responsibility and, 3

thriving. *See also Surviving, Striving, and Thriving* framework
  Ali on, 74
  career as, 49
  defined, 34, 43
  Lamar on, 74
  Malcolm on, 74
  orientation towards, 52
  transformative change needed, 90

Us versus Them, 3–4

visual pathways
  Cedric, 58
  ideas for use of, 99
  Lamar, 60
  Lukas, 63
  Lyrik, 30
  Malcolm, 81
  Maria, 25
  overview, 16–17
  Renee, 21
  research dissemination using, 93
  Xavier, 55
vocational education, benefits of, xi–xii
vocational identity, as underexplored, xii. *See also* occupational identity development
voices
  anecdotal presentation of, 10–11, 14
  devaluation of those of young people, 5–6
  elevating youth, 85–86, 91–93, 96, 110
  importance of listening to, 13–17, 74–75, 97
  not losing when aggregating data, ix
  power of, 9–12

white supremacy, 89
word choice for self-description, 95
work. *See also* careers; jobs
    assumptions of adults about, 56
    desire to like, 24–25, 27
    focus group view of, 46–48
    as means to end, 36–37

Xavier
    barriers for, 67
    on careers, 49
    introduction of, 42
    on jobs, 44
    pathway for, 54–57
    on racism, 69, 70

    reflections on focus group, 82, 83
    self-description, 68

young people. *See also* Black young people; *specific participants by name*
    adults having limited interaction with, 9–10
    advisory panels of, 93
    immersion with, 10–12
    voices of needing to be elevated, 5–6, 85–86, 91–93, 96, 110
Youth, Education, and the Role of Society (Halpern), xi–xii
youth advisory panels (YAP), 93